BANK ON SELF-INVESTMENT

BELIEF DEPOSITED—TRIUMPH WITHDRAWN

A STIMULUS CHECK FOR ONE'S SELF

Written by
MICHAEL D. LEWIS

Copyright © 2020 by Michael Dane Lewis
All rights reserved.

ISBN: 9780578787312
ISBN-13: 978-0-578-78731-2

This book is copyright protected.

You cannot amend, distribute, sell, use, quote, or paraphrase any part of this book—except for brief quotations in critical reviews or articles—without consent from the author or publisher.
No warranties of any kind are declared or implied. Readers acknowledge that the author is not engaged in rendering legal, financial, or professional advice. Consult a licensed professional if legal or expert services are needed.

Self-published through
MT INSIGNIA 2.0 LLC

PRINTED IN THE UNITED STATES OF AMERICA

Cover Design by Ryan Biore | Ryanurz
Interior Design by Ultimate Book Formatting
Author Photo by Maria Kandalova Photography LLC

To my grandmother, Ivy May Landells-Lewis...
...for guiding me under her wings of wisdom.
To all individuals who want to increase in value and lead others.
To my immediate and extended family.
To all my friends.
To self!

"Be there for others, but never leave yourself behind."

— DODINSKY

CONTENTS

Preface   vii
Acknowledgments   xi
Introduction   xiii

Part I
DEPOSITING BELIEF

1. Self-Realization   3
   Articulate Yourself As An "Investment Account"

2. Self-Evaluation   12
   You Are Your "Prospectus"

3. Self-Regulation   27
   Valuing Self-Investment "Assets" And "Collaterals"

4. Self-Confidence   38
   "Depositing" Belief In Yourself

5. Self-Reliance   53
   You Are The "Beneficiary" Of Your Self-Investment

Part II
WITHDRAWING TRIUMPH

6. Self-Determination   69
   Acquiring Developmental "Dividends"

7. Self-Efficacy   80
   "Overdrafting" On Your Potential To Build Self-Worth

8. Self-Awareness   92
   "Capitalizing" On Creativity

9. Self-Construction   102
   Avoiding Moral "Bankruptcy" And Acts Of "Fraud"

10. Self-Trust   116
    Recouping From Failed Personal "Transactions"

Part III
SELF-UPGRADE IN PROGRESS...

11. **Self-Care** 129
    Your Self-Investment "Agenda" Guide

12. **Self-Made** 146
    Drafting Your "Self-Investment Statement"

13. **Self-Upgrade** 156
    "Withdrawing" From Recurring Accounts Of Success

Conclusion 161

References 167

PREFACE

April 2020

It's been a long time coming, but the 2019 Coronavirus disease (COVID-19) evolved from an isolated virus in a region of China to a pandemic that not only has engulfed the nations of the world, it has also exposed a great need for us as individuals to reassess ourselves. Governments worldwide have spent several billions of dollars on stimulus packages in light of the loss of individuals' livelihoods and depreciation of countries' prosperity. Their aim was to forestall economic free-fall, but the pandemic caused the usual operation of business to come to a grinding halt.

Lockdown! Standstill! Quarantine! Curfew!

Stimulus Check! Squander! Idle!

Wait! Nothing!

Hmm, I remember thinking.

The real stimulus check that people need today is one of self-assessment. This is the structural thought that first led me to outline the framework of this book. *But how can I make it more interesting and engaging?* I thought to myself. After a few days of critical thinking, I finally decided on using banking and investment metaphors to drive the comprehension of the philosophies and tactics I outlined.

My thought process continued. Now is the time for us to endure a robust kind of formative evaluation to explicitly reflect on and assess how we plan to tackle the adventures of attaining the quality of life we envision for ourselves.

In my judgment, the global economy can be strongly rebuilt if each person focuses on constructing their personal economy—those things that allow us to flourish in our individualized beacon of greatness.

Every day, you miss out on dozens of opportunities to improve your life. These opportunities might slip past you completely unnoticed. Or worse, you decide to let them pass you by because you are too afraid to reach out and grab them. This book utilizes a mixture of banking and investment jargons to theorize and explain novel self-investment concepts metaphorically. It is carefully crafted to help you gain a broader perspective of—and a deeper understanding into—who you are and how you envision yourself. It is *"A Stimulus Check for One's Self"* because it will challenge you to perform practical actions that can allow you to gain momentum on your life's goals.

Are you someone who feels too scared by the possibility of failure to put yourself out there? Are you reluctant to put your skills to the test because you don't feel like they're good enough yet? Are you clueless about your goals, to the point where you don't recognize just how valuable even one of these opportunities could be in changing your life for the better? If you're someone who shies away from change and lives your life too afraid of failure to take a shot at success, then learning how to invest in yourself can change your life for the better.

Investing isn't just useful for banks and stock markets. You can also invest in your future success. Self-investment encourages you to consider your long-term goals. Where do you want to be in five years? What about ten? Are you doing everything you can to ensure you achieve your goals, or could you be doing much more?

When you invest in yourself, you view yourself the same way you would consider a financial investment. You want to get the highest possible return on your investment, and you can only do that by cultivating the traits, skills, and mentality you need to succeed. A little bit of investment now ensures you will have a much greater reward later, and any work you put in will be well worth the effort when you are living the life you've always dreamed of. Begin by investing belief in yourself, and eventually, you will be able to withdraw triumph.

In *"Bank on Self-Investment,"* you will learn:

- Why you need to start investing in yourself sooner rather than later
- What it means to deposit positive qualities, like belief and hard work, and what you can gain by doing so
- How you can make an incredible amount of progress toward

your goals by developing your skills and taking your future seriously

A bank account only grows in value when you deposit money into it. You must make the initial investment—and the sooner, the better. The earlier you start investing in yourself, the more time your investment will have to generate interest, and the more life-changing your results will be.

The best time to start self-investing is right now. When you bank on self-investment, you are sure to increase your self-worth, and then some.

ACKNOWLEDGMENTS

Writing this book proved to be one of my most challenging yet rewarding milestones. This accomplishment would not have been possible without aid from God and several people.

I'm eternally grateful to my granny, Ivy May Landells-Lewis. She taught me several life lessons that helped me sow seeds of belief in myself. Now, I am reaping the rewards of my labor. I cannot imagine where I'd be if she had not accepted me and provided a roof over my head when I was less than a year old.

It is an incredible pleasure to meet people who are genuinely invested in the growth and development of others. My gratitude knows no bounds in expressing thanks to Dr. Jeffrey Emmerich, one of my Fine Arts Professors, whose encouragement fueled my motivation to write this book. His email on March 10, 2019, said:

> "Michael, I recommend that you copy your emails (such as this perfectly penned one...) and keep them in a folder. Your writing style is (dare I say) superior to most students I encounter, and I predict that one day you will be [a] writer. Seriously. Your command of the English language is stunning. I'm very proud of you."
>
> — JE

I'm forever indebted to my English Professor, Olivia Buzzacco, for her editorial help, thoughtful insights, and constant support as a friend. To all my other friends who helped select the perfect cover for this book, thank you. If I undertook this process alone, I would have plucked each strand of hair from my head—one by one.

I want to acknowledge my international academic sponsors, Carolyn Meana and OBX Lighthouse Church, for prolonging my agonies with continual encouragement and flexible support. Thank you for being loyal supporters of my academic and professional pursuits.

Finally, to my family in The Cayman Islands and Jamaica, and the Landells and Ryce families in America, I appreciate you all.

Their motivations certainly allowed me to endure the process of writing this book to help others become better versions of themselves.

INTRODUCTION

My relatives, close friends, and acquaintances often ask me why I am so resilient and unwavering in my dedication to accomplishing my goals. They wonder how I manage to remain persistent in the face of hardship and how this persistence allows me to succeed. My answer to them is always the same: *I am my most significant investment. If I don't invest in myself first, no one else will!*

Investing in yourself and developing resilience go hand in hand—they are inseparable. If you want to remain resilient against any challenge life throws at you and come out the other side victorious, you need to cultivate this mindset. Without dedication and commitment, you will have difficulty achieving the goals that matter most to you. Self-investment is just like any other kind of investment: you get out of it what you put in. When you make smart investments, whether you're investing money or you're investing time and energy in yourself, the payoff you receive will be well worth the initial effort.

Investing can be tricky, especially if you're a beginner. It's intimidating to spend money without any guarantee that you will get anything in return. Besides, you know there's always the risk you might not get your money back. The knowledge of this risk can give you such intense anxiety about investing that you choose to avoid it altogether. However, while deciding not to invest at all means there is no chance of losing your money, it also means you cannot gain any money either. Hence, if you cannot commit to investing a small portion of your earnings now, reaping financial rewards later down the line is impossible.

Choosing to invest in yourself follows the same principle. Success is not guaranteed, but you cannot grow as a person and increase your chances of succeeding in life unless you are willing to make an effort first. Self-investment involves developing good habits and a positive, achievement-oriented attitude. It means cultivating good traits in yourself and improving yourself in order to increase the likelihood of future success. As you teach yourself critical life skills like determination, resilience, focus, and a desire to learn and see yourself become a better and more capable person, you will develop a forward-thinking mindset. This positive attitude and thirst for growth will equip you to handle and endure the onslaught of difficulties you might experience in life.

Self-investment is also inextricably linked to the idea of finding satisfaction in your life. Investing in yourself allows you to feel a genuine connection to your happiness as you get a better understanding of what you want in life and how you can achieve it. Finding peace in what you choose to do with your life allows you to feel more fulfilled, and this newfound peace also gives you the motivation needed to work toward your highest ambitions.

Self-investment is not always easy, but the benefits are well worth any challenges you might encounter. You are full of untapped potential. Right now, it might be hard to see all the fantastic things you can do in your lifetime. You might worry about whether you will ever amount to anything or make a difference in the lives of others, or the world at large. But if you keep improving and always strive to be a little better, you can keep getting closer and closer to your goals. You will develop the skills you need to follow through on your life's ambitions. You will also become better at navigating personal relationships. Without self-investment, you run the risk of failing to improve your skills. This failure to invest in yourself could lead to missed opportunities and regrets. Worse, if you don't recognize how crucial continual improvement is, you might lack the motivation to chase your dreams. Giving up on your goals is the worst thing you can do because it keeps you from ever knowing if you could have accomplished them. You have the potential for greatness, but you will have a lot of trouble achieving it if you don't spend time investing in yourself first. For all these reasons, you can—and should—bank on self-investment.

One typical stumbling block for self-investment is a tendency to put others' needs above your own. Are you the type of person who pays a lot of attention to how others feel at the expense of your feelings? Do you find yourself going out of your way to agree with others even when you disagree? Have you ever done a favor for someone even though you had a packed schedule that left you scrambling to finish your work? This kind of situation is very common if you're someone who has trouble putting your own needs first. It's great to want to help others, but this should never happen at your own expense.

I know first-hand exactly how taxing this pattern of behavior can be. In the past, my problem—not quite the worst problem in a sense—was that I would always put others' desires above my own. I wanted to help my friends and family, but I didn't realize that I was neglecting my individual needs in the process. I spent a significant portion of my time working on projects for others, which meant I ended up procrastinating my own work. In the end, I either failed to finish personal assignments on time or ended up working on them late at night, frantically trying to complete them before I fell asleep in the middle of my attempt. This selfless lifestyle wasn't a healthy way to live, and it was causing me to experience near-constant burnout.

The mistake I made, which is the same mistake you have also likely made, was sacrificing my own time and energy to invest in others when I should have been investing in myself first. Often, the work I did for others would come out worse than I intended—as would my own. Instead of helping a friend, I overburdened myself and ended up dragging both of us down. Think of what they tell you in airplanes about putting on your oxygen mask before helping others with theirs. If you try to put an oxygen mask on someone else first, you might both pass out before either of you are wearing one. If you see to your needs and responsibilities first, then you can help others. Better yet, your help will often be much more effective because you have prior experience, which allows you to execute the job correctly.

In this regard, my wake-up call emanated after reading a blog post that explained the oxygen-mask complex I used previously. The post said I needed to satisfy my own needs and invest in myself first and foremost. Whether I wanted to develop myself professionally and personally, improve a skill I already had, learn a brand-new skill, or start making healthier lifestyle choices, I needed to give to myself first. It is only after working on myself that I could give to others or expect others to give to me. I needed to start helping myself first so that I could improve my lot in life and have a better position from which to help others.

This book contains all the lessons I have learned about the importance of self-investment. It is a blueprint for stoking the flames of your inner fire and turning self-improvement into success. Reading this book will help you understand what you want out of life, teach you how to set goals that align with your dreams, and educate you on the skills and behaviors needed to pursue those dreams. It is *"A Stimulus Check for One's Self"* because it will give you a greater sense of all the amazing things you can do once you start investing in yourself, and challenge you to perform practical actions that can allow you to gain momentum on your life's goals.

You can learn more, do more, and achieve more, but all your efforts must stem from a desire to improve yourself.

I am living proof of just how powerful self-investment can be. I was born in Jamaica, where I was raised by my grandmother, Ivy May Landells-Lewis, who taught me several valuable life lessons that made me a better human. From my grandmother, I gained a strong desire to abandon mediocrity and strive for something more. Ivy motivated me not just to have faith in myself, but also to help others overcome their fear of doing and their lack of belief in themselves. Her prudent wisdom and relentless encouragement ultimately shaped me into the person I am today.

Furthermore, my participation in extracurricular activities in school and interaction with experts in various fields triggered my curiosity about self-investment and helped me bank on my capabilities. Those experiences taught me to prioritize my personal growth and development, and through this, I have acquired an in-depth understanding of personal enrichment. This constant desire to continuously improve myself helps me reap the rewards that flourish from the genuine belief that I cyclically deposit in myself. Now, my go-to ritual is investing in my emotional and physical well-being while also constructing my personal and professional lives, so they reflect what I want to get out of life.

I will guide you on how to develop the same rituals to improve your chances of success.

Investing in yourself is the first step toward living a more personally fulfilling life. You need to identify your goals and give yourself the tools and resources necessary to achieve them. Investing in yourself is just as important as investing in your bank account. You put a little money in now, and the amount of money in your account will continue to increase over time. The effort you expend will pay dividends later. When you bank on self-investment, you bank on a better future for yourself.

Your skill sets and talents are worth investing in; they are assets that will never decrease in value. When you purposefully work on yourself to *grow* and *glow* as a better person, don't think of it as an expense—it is an incredible investment you're making.

Your stimulus check starts now!

I

DEPOSITING BELIEF

1

SELF-REALIZATION
ARTICULATE YOURSELF AS AN "INVESTMENT ACCOUNT"

Envisioning yourself as an investment account will allow you to grow in value purposefully.

Self-realization will bring you more fulfillment than anything else in life. You can pack your life full of simple pleasures and immediate gratification from sugary food, TV, and video games, but if this is all your life is, you may never truly feel complete. If you don't have a purpose you're working toward, you will definitely feel as though your life is entirely directionless.

Self-realization is simply the point at which you have fulfilled your potential. It happens when you allow yourself to dream up the best possible life for you, and then you follow through on that dream. You might spend a good portion of your life working toward your highest aspirations—the best things in life take some effort to achieve, after all. But as long as you feel like you've identified your purpose, and you're making progress toward that purpose, it is easier to feel that your life has meaning and you are on the path to greatness.

How can you work toward and achieve self-realization? There are so many people who live their lives without purpose. When they are old and gray, they will look back on their lives and wonder why they didn't do more to uplift themselves as they got older. You don't want this to be you, but how do you avoid it? The key lies in learning to see yourself and your time as an investment you make for a better future. Put in the work now so you can see amazing results later.

From time to time, I consciously reflect on the experiences I had as a teenager. When I was attending Denbigh High School in Clarendon, Jamaica, I was either distracted by one thing or another, lost in my thoughts, or overwhelmed by grim emotions. Distractions came in various forms; however, I was mostly distracted from my studies because I was a member of a majority of the clubs and societies my school offered. There were also times when negative thoughts penetrated my mind and crippled my ability to thrive in school among the top performers. I was uncertain of my sense of belonging to the point where my most difficult emotions caused me to consider weakening my quest for greatness. I ruminated over the implications of the decisions I had already made, and the ones I contemplated doing.

I was engaging in what Mrs. Parchment, one of my guidance counselors at the time, delineated as self-realization. For me, it was a proactive enlightenment that caused me to visualize progression toward induced self-development by harnessing my talents and skills, amidst my internal struggles. This was a regeneration phase in my life. Herein, I envisioned a profound life change, for the better, that intuitively propelled me to invest time and effort into elevating myself. Later, I significantly reduced the stress and anxiety associated with being in high school. Michael Dane Lewis was now perceived as an investment account. Literally, the very first account I ever owned. The dire need to nourish my knowledge, confidence, and creativity stemmed from a place of self-love. I began to understand myself and the value I had to offer my institution as I commenced my self-development quest.

Articulating yourself as an investment account lies at the very heart of self-realization. Because I saw myself as an investment account, I deposited the necessary dues out of respect to see myself grow abundantly. I became more focused on a brighter tomorrow, and I gained control over my emotions. My self-awareness, self-esteem, and self-confidence skyrocketed. This mindset helped me pave a path to success, as I genuinely understood that significant profits lie ahead when investments are aligned with specific goals from the get-go.

If you want to become an accomplished individual, you ought to start looking at yourself as an investment account for your future success. Envisioning yourself as an investment account will allow you to grow in value purposefully. By imagining yourself as an investment account today, you will eventually form a brighter and more positive future for yourself; you will invest in your future with the knowledge that it will pay off. Proper planning and self-investment now help pave the way to success.

PAVING THE WAY TO SUCCESS

It's incredibly hard to achieve success in life without a clear plan for what you want to do. Very rarely do people trip and fall into success. More often than not, success is the product of a lot of hard work stretched out over a few years, with things set in motion early on and paying off years later. For example, you could think of graduating from high school as an early investment you make in yourself. When you graduate, you open up many pathways for continued education that were previously closed off to you. You might not see the fruits of your labor the second you graduate, but you will in the future. If you don't make this early investment, you don't get the satisfaction of a future payoff.

Since self-investment is all about the idea of improving your future, you want to take a long-term view of your life goals. Don't just focus on what you can achieve right now. Start to think about what you could achieve months or years into the future if you put your mind to it. When you start thinking long-term, it becomes easier to figure out what investments you can make right now to help you reach your goals. You can achieve self-realization, but first, you need to make specific plans.

THE VALUE OF PLANNING

Investments are not something people rush into, whether they're financial or even personal. For financial investments, you need to know what you're doing before you invest your money. Otherwise, you could be wasting your money without any big payoff. Investing in yourself works the same way. If you don't devise a clear plan of action and you're unsure of what you're trying to achieve, you're going to have to rely heavily on luck to make something out of your life, and that just isn't reliable enough. Just as investors need to know the market they're investing in and their personal goals, you need to know what you should focus on in order to achieve your version of success.

Let's say one of your goals is that you want to get a job as a doctor. There are many smaller steps involved in this process. You will need to do some research to figure out the education requirements for doctors in your area. You may have to attend a specific university or take a particular exam. If you want to get accepted to an exceptionally competitive university with a highly rated Medical Science program, you will more than likely need to do well in college to be a good candidate for that program. Each of these steps should be part of your plan to become a doctor eventually. If you don't take the time to establish this plan, however, you might not realize just how early you need to start investing in yourself, or you could invest in the wrong things. It is only through planning that you can guarantee that you will make the best self-investment decisions.

SETTING GOALS

Part of planning is learning how to set goals for yourself. If you are trying to achieve self-realization, you need to take some time to figure out precisely what self-realization means to you. What goals really matter to you? If you could achieve absolutely anything, what would it be? Setting goals gives you something clear and concrete to work toward; when you know exactly what would make you feel fulfilled, it becomes much easier to figure out what kind of investments you need to make in yourself to get there.

Remember that your goals should prioritize the things you care about most, which means they should have substantial personal value. Many people choose their careers according to what would make them the most money, and while it's okay to want to have money, it's more powerful to consider why you want a well-paying job. Do you want to be able to support your family? Do you want financial freedom that allows you to explore other passions and hobbies outside of work? Do you genuinely care about the good work and positive impact you would be making on the job? If you pick a job just because it pays well and you don't actually like the job, you're probably not going to feel fulfilled. Many people end up going back to school or even dropping out of college because they lived their life for someone else. They made an investment in the future someone else wanted them to have, not the one they wanted for themselves, which meant a lot of their initial investment didn't pay off the way they hoped it would. You don't want this to happen, so try to choose goals that align with your aspirations.

Of course, that's not to say your goals can never change. The chances are that when you were younger, your answer to "What do you want to be when you grow up?" was significantly different from what it is now. This uncertainty of a clear direction for your life is perfectly fine. As you grow older and learn much more about yourself, your interests might change too. Even though you might have spent some time working toward a goal that no longer appeals to you, this effort wasn't in vain. You still probably learned valuable life skills—like resolve and self-confidence—that apply to your new goal. It's like discovering your true passion in college and switching majors. In addition to the plethora of new courses you're now taking to obtain a different degree, the previous courses taken will help you to gain a broader perspective of the world around you. Essentially, the classes that your college deems unnecessary to earn your newly targeted degree will still be applicable in your daily life. Every one of them becomes necessary! This analogy is to reiterate the point that you ought to re-invest learned skills toward accomplishing any new goal you decide to tackle. As long as you are continually investing in yourself and aiming to become a better, more accomplished person, there is no such thing as wasted effort.

INVEST TODAY, PROFIT TOMORROW

We've mentioned treating yourself like an investment account, but what does this actually mean? To answer the question, we'll need to take a closer look at what exactly an investment account is.

When you first start investing, you will need to set up an investment account for yourself. These are also called brokerage accounts. Unlike a standard bank account, an investment account allows you to make additional money by investing the funds you put into the account in stocks, bonds, and mutual funds. Therefore, your investment account is the initial commitment you make toward investing in the stock market.

In the realm of self-investment, you are the investment account. You provide the reserves of energy and dedication you will need in order to start investing. An investment account is all about commitment to making a change in your life, whether that change is personal or financial. Through this commitment, you hold yourself accountable for achieving future success.

Your investment account is the foundation upon which all of your efforts are built. Give yourself a solid foundation through planning and goal setting, and you will make things easier for yourself later on. By doing this, you are laying the groundwork that will pay off in the future; the initial investment you will follow through on as you start developing and improving your personal and professional skills.

MAKING INVESTMENTS THAT ALIGN WITH YOUR GOALS

Setting goals is so important because it gives you a sense of direction. When you know what you want to achieve, it is easier to plan out how you will work toward achieving it. The investments you make should align with the results you want to see. This is as true for your financial investments as it is for self-investment.

There are many different kinds of investment accounts, each of which helps investors achieve a different goal. Breaking investment accounts into different categories with varied purposes makes it easier to choose an investment plan that feels right for your needs. For example, some investment accounts are used exclusively for retirement funds. These kinds of investments tend to make less money over time, but they are safer. If you're retiring, you don't want to end up losing all of your saved money, so safe investments are essential.

On the other hand, standard brokerage accounts can be a little riskier, but they tend to reap greater rewards. Some people use investment accounts tailored for specific purposes, such as education accounts, which help pay for education expenses and can only be paid out toward eligible schools. Each of these accounts serves a different purpose; they help investors achieve their respective goals.

Investing in yourself should follow the same idea. Choose investments that bring you closer to your goals. If you want to get a job that requires a degree, you will need to invest in your education. Depending on the job, this could mean focusing on one area of study over another, or it might mean getting a well-rounded education. You might need to learn specific skills depending on what you're trying to achieve too. Someone who wants to run their own business will need different skills than someone who wants to climb through the ranks at their current job. The same is true for various hobbies. The skills a painter learns are different than those a writer learns and very different from those an athlete learns. You will also need to invest in developing interpersonal skills if your goals involve forming meaningful personal relationships. Knowing your goals allows you to tailor your investment plan accordingly.

When you start looking at yourself as an investment account, you start noticing how the actions you take affect how close you are to achieving your goals. Activities that encourage self-investment in the right areas bring you closer to success, while procrastinating work and neglecting self-development make it harder to succeed. As you start to pick up on these trends, it becomes easier to make the right decisions and purposefully increase your value.

2

SELF-EVALUATION
YOU ARE YOUR "PROSPECTUS"

Creating a substantial self-prospectus by way of critical self-evaluation elevates your confidence to outline feasible goals and motivates you to accomplish them.

To improve anything, you need to begin by examining your starting position. If you want to grow a garden, you need to take stock of the soil quality and any plants that are already growing in the area. If you want to achieve a specific grade in school, you need to examine your current grades alongside the curriculum to become aware of what areas need the most improvement. If you want to improve yourself, you need to perform an honest evaluation of where you are now. This evaluation will help you decide what kind of changes you want to make in order to improve and uplift yourself.

In finance, the document that gives potential investors information about a company's investment security status is known as a prospectus. It is a legal document prepared by companies, and it contains in-depth details about a mutual fund, stock, bond, or other investments. This document typically includes information about how many shares are being offered by a company, a background on the company, and its financial status, among other things, so investors can know if the stock being offered is a good match (Kuffel, 2019, para. 3). It takes some of the uncertainty out of the process of investing by giving investors more information about how well a company is doing right now. With this information, investors can decide if investing in the company is a good fit for their goals, and the magnitude of risk tolerance they're comfortable with.

When you're investing in yourself, you must perform a self-evaluation and create a prospectus too. You need a sense of where your starting point is. Do you have a long way to go before you meet your goals, or are there just a handful of things you need to change? How far away are you from where you want to be in life? What have you done so far to get closer to your goals, and what do you still need to do? Answering these questions will help you get a better sense of your "personal prospectus."

At Denbigh High School, every exam season hit me with a tidal wave of depression. No matter how hard I tried to prepare for those exams, the Bs, Cs, and Ds always presented themselves on my report card—every term. At that point in my academic life, my prospectus was not looking very good. Some of the actual comments on my report cards were:

"Michael is capable of doing better, but he needs to give his school work greater priority."

"A fair performance, but [he] needs to settle down and exert more effort."

"Capable student, but he wastes time. He needs to be more focused."

"[He] tries, but seems to find the subject difficult."

One teacher even wrote, "A disappointing exam result."

This was unsatisfying. I wanted to rip my report cards into a million pieces to erase the evidence of my academic dissatisfaction. Though my grandmother, father, and other relatives were constantly disappointed in my academic performance in high school, they believed I could do better and continuously motivated me to try to do so. To be honest, I just wanted to ditch classes. No. I wanted to stay home, but I wouldn't be allowed to. I found it very hard to sit in classes and face my teachers, knowing they showed me up like that to my guardians. But, I had no other choice. I needed to learn and prove to everyone that I was really capable of performing better.

In the fifth form, leading up to the Caribbean Secondary Education Certificate (CSEC) examinations, I underwent a period of self-evaluation.

How do I recover from these near-failing and failing grades and flourish on the CSEC exams?

Can my aim of becoming Head Boy or Deputy Head Boy—roles of prominent student responsibility used in the British education system —*be accomplished if I do not perform well on the CSEC exams?*

What can I do to ensure that I get good enough grades to transition to university smoothly?

Receiving bad grades on the CSEC exams could be devastating in several ways. I realized that if I did not perform well enough on those exams, the chances were I would have to re-sit them, and that would impede my aim to become the next Head Boy or Deputy Head Boy. On top of those possible outcomes, failing those exams would also hamper my goal to attend university sooner, rather than later.

The self-evaluation I performed propelled me to shift my attention to what was necessary at the time—my academics. Achieving better grades was at the top of my priorities in the latter part of fifth form. At that time, my in-class grade for Mathematics was C, and I had a D in English. The other subjects did not look so good either, except for a few. My interest was in the Arts. I had an A in Visual Arts. Moreover, my passion for acting led me to pursue Theater Arts as an additional CSEC subject as if I had not enough burden with nine others. To study this subject alone, I was required to travel on the weekends to another high school—Mona High School in Kingston, Jamaica— roughly an hour-and-a-half drive away from my hometown.

The high level of commitment I exerted to ensure that my grades improved caused me to ignore prior distractions. My participation in extracurricular activities and the time I would spend hanging out with friends decreased drastically. The hours I spent reading, writing, and practicing in preparation for my exams increased significantly. I devoted myself to preparing for the level of stress I would endure during every external exam. My mind was set on entering each sitting with confidence and exiting just the same.

In the end, I was successful in all my CSEC examinations. For Theater Arts, I was the top-performing student in Jamaica, and I was ranked fourth in the Caribbean. I was admitted to sixth form and assigned the positions of Deputy Head Boy and Peer Counselor President. Two years later, I was qualified to enroll in any Jamaican university. As I assessed my performance on high school exams, I underwent a more in-depth evaluation of myself and the goals I envisioned achieving. At that time in my life, I realized that those goals, and several others, were far-fetched if good grades were not part of my prospectus.

In a sense, you are your prospectus. Your self-evaluation and commitment to positive change let others know you are serious about your success. They can put their faith in you confidently. Think of this as a job interview. In the interview, you present your prospectus, which tells a potential employer your background and how you've improved. If your prospectus is strong, the employer knows there is minimal risk in hiring you. They can be sure you're going to get the job done well, all because you invested in yourself and improved your prospectus. That said, your prospectus isn't just for others to be amazed by you and your accomplishments. It helps you have faith in yourself as well. Creating a substantial self-prospectus by way of critical self-evaluation elevates your confidence to outline feasible goals and motivates you to accomplish them.

WHY SELF-EVALUATION IS CRITICAL FOR SELF-INVESTMENT

Self-evaluation is a foundational step in self-investment. You want to have a solid grasp on where you're starting from so you can create a clear path toward what you want to achieve. Self-evaluation makes it much easier to fill in the blank steps between where you are and where you want to end up.

While self-evaluation is necessary, it's not always easy. No one wants to feel as though they are doing something wrong, and it can be hard to realize just how much work you might need to put in before you are ready to achieve your goals. However, it is still a worthwhile endeavor when you're developing your prospectus. Performing a personal inventory lets you locate any problems that could interfere with your chances of success before they can get in your way. If you don't recognize a problem exists, it may be incredibly challenging to fix it. This is the same reason why your boss might give you an employee evaluation. Bosses don't evaluate employees to be mean; employees are evaluated to highlight areas where they can improve, alongside areas they are already excelling in. This review helps employees become better and more efficient at their job. Self-evaluation serves the same purpose. It not only gives you a realistic idea of where you're having trouble and where your self-investment would be most beneficial, but it also highlights what you're doing right. When you evaluate yourself, you take the first steps toward becoming the best possible version of yourself.

TAKING A LONG-TERM VIEW OF YOUR LIFE

Delayed gratification is an often-overlooked skill. It's very easy to get caught up in the moment and only focus on how your actions impact you right at that second. You might think that pursuing a skill isn't worth it because you will never become good enough at it. On the other hand, you might do something you know is bad for you because it brings you instant gratification, justifying it by saying you're only doing it once. The truth is that when you shift your focus from a short-term view to a long-term one, you start to see how each little action you take adds up. Practicing a skill for half an hour one day isn't going to immediately make you amazing at it, but if you can delay your gratification a little and keep practicing every day, you will become much better at the skill. Procrastinating work for one day might not be so bad, but if you keep doing it, you're going to have a lot of trouble keeping up with your responsibilities in the long term. You will end up doing more work than you would have if you'd practiced delayed gratification from the outset and started the work on time.

The habits we engage in every day add up to a much larger whole. For example, if you have a single slice of cake one day, that's okay. However, if you have cake multiple times in a month, that single slice of cake becomes much more of an issue. If you get into a habit of eating cake, your health will suffer, even though it initially seemed harmless. Good habits are sure to pay off in the future, while bad ones are sure to cause problems for you.

Self-evaluation helps you see the potential of every action you take. When you examine where you are in life and how you got here, you begin to grasp how your actions helped to construct the person you are today. You also get a sense of how you can use self-investment to replace bad habits with good ones, always keeping in mind the long-term results of your choices. Investing in yourself is a good habit. You can start now to encourage future success. Self-evaluation will help you invest in yourself efficiently, because it allows you to identify the patterns and practices that are most likely to bring about positive change in your life. When you look toward the future instead of living in the moment, you can reap greater rewards and avoid falling prey to instant gratification.

BRINGING YOUR GOALS INTO FOCUS

You cannot "set and forget" your goals. If you want to make progress toward them, you always need to know what you are trying to achieve. Forgetting your goals and pushing them aside means you're not putting in any work, and you're not investing in yourself. You're not engaging in the constructive habits that will bring you closer to success. Thinking about your goals more often plants a seed in your subconscious mind. So, you start making choices that will help you make progress toward your goals, even if you don't notice it at the time. You're more likely to take opportunities presented to you instead of letting them pass you by. In short, you become a more proactive person.

Self-evaluation keeps your goals at the forefront of your mind at all times. It lets you assess yourself and see how close you are to your goals, and it encourages you to make the necessary changes to bring you even closer. When you evaluate your progress regularly, you keep checking in on yourself, creating accountability for your self-improvement. This helps you stay motivated and keeps you on the right track.

ELIMINATING GUESSWORK

A company's prospectus helps potential investors answer questions they might have about how risky a particular stock is or what kind of return on investment they can expect. If you look only at the current price of a stock, you won't know much about it. You might be able to say whether the price is good or bad, but you don't have any idea if the stock has gone up in value in the last few months or if it's only decreased over time. You also don't know if the stock price has stayed relatively consistent or if it tends to fluctuate wildly. The prospectus provides the necessary context for a stock. It contains background information that can help potential buyers make a more accurate prediction about a stock's future potential. It takes the guesswork out of purchasing stocks and helps investors decide if their investment is worth it or not.

Self-evaluation serves a similar purpose. While self-investment isn't nearly as risky as investing in stocks—because you will always benefit from improving yourself—you still want to have a good idea of your background in the context of your goals. Consider what you have done so far to get closer to your goals and what you need to continue to do. Also, use self-evaluation as a resource to identify the skills and experiences you need to achieve your ambitions. Using this time to re-evaluate your past and plan for the future means you won't have to guess what your next steps should be as you keep working toward your goal. You only need to follow the plan you have already laid out for yourself.

HOW TO EVALUATE YOURSELF

You now know why self-evaluation is so essential, but how do you go about performing one? First, you must know what categories you're evaluating yourself on. This requires you to understand your goals so you can measure your progress toward them. Decide what would qualify as excelling in each goal and keep your goals measurable whenever possible. For example, a nonspecific goal like "get better grades in school" is hard to succeed at, as you haven't identified what "better" means. Do you want to improve by just a few grade points, or do you have a specific goal in mind? It is more helpful to give yourself a specific target, like trying to achieve a particular grade in each class. This approach will allow you to know precisely when you've accomplished that goal. It also means you will have an easier time measuring your progress and deciding if your habits will help or hurt your ability to achieve each goal you set out to accomplish.

Your self-evaluation will be most effective if you go into it with the right mentality. Looking at yourself with an assessing eye isn't always easy, especially if you tend to either think of yourself too critically or not critically enough. Finding a balance between these two extremes is tough, but it's absolutely necessary for a useful self-evaluation. It will allow you to become a more introspective person, not to mention a more goal-oriented one. Here are a few things to keep in mind when you're evaluating yourself.

PRACTICE SELF-REFLECTION

Self-reflection helps you understand the areas where you most need to grow. It gives you a complete picture of not just who you are, but also who you could be if you set your mind to it. Self-reflection is necessary for creating and following through on goals, but it is also great because it lets you feel more in tune with yourself. When you understand yourself fully, you become more conscious of your choices and the impact they have on you and others.

Take time to think about what each day teaches you, and how you can use your experiences to grow as a person. Slow down and encourage yourself to become more mindful of your habits. Think before you act, and reflect on any actions you do take. One study about self-reflection revealed that "employees who spent 15 minutes at the end of the day reflecting about lessons learned performed 23% better after 10 days than those who did not reflect" (Porter, 2017, para. 4). This is a significant change that is only made possible through introspection. Undeniably, employees who contribute more to a company's productivity are those who engage in some form of work-related self-reflection.

Interestingly, my acting instructor at the College of The Albemarle, Professor Krueger, continues to encourage her students to develop a culture of reflective practices after each seminar class. In one of her classes, she logically explained that critical thinking and memorization stem from reflecting—profoundly analyzing what you've learned from the concepts, theories, and ideas communicated. You can extend this concept far beyond work and school into almost every aspect of your life. If you want to become more productive and a lot more effective, you need to make self-reflection part of your evaluation strategy.

IDENTIFY AREAS IN NEED OF IMPROVEMENT

Think of self-evaluation as a method for understanding your strengths and weaknesses. Use it to get an idea of what you're already doing right and what you need to change to become more successful. Think about times when you feel you might have mishandled a situation, or when you weren't able to make the most of an opportunity because you lacked the proper skills. These are areas that you can invest in to experience the most significant increase in your potential. Next time one of these opportunities comes along, your self-investment will ensure that you are ready to take advantage of it. No evaluation is complete without allowing yourself an opportunity to improve. Besides, you can't efficaciously progress if you're not willing to be truthful about aspects of yourself that need to change.

This process is, understandably, not always easy. It can feel like you're only putting yourself down, and if you already struggle with self-esteem issues, it can be even more challenging. Changing the way you think about self-evaluation might make it easier to do. Everyone has room to grow, and taking time to identify areas you can improve in isn't something to be ashamed of. You shouldn't be trying to maliciously criticize yourself or make yourself feel bad for past actions; instead, your evaluation should help you focus on the future. You have the power to change any part of yourself that's holding you back, whether it's a particular skill that you lack or a poor mindset that inhibits your ability to grow.

On October 4, 2020, I was late for church because I took part in a press interview for longer than I expected. However, I was on time to hear an important part of the message, dubbed "Seven Habits: Meditation." In discussing the habit of having a concrete mindset, Pastor Chris Wilson said:

"Your mindset will determine...who you are. It will determine what you can do as well as what you do. And it also determines what you will have. Your mindset—the thoughts [and] ideas that you are operating by—will determine your outlook in life, which in turn, will determine everything else."

On this note, when you start thinking of yourself as someone capable of improving, any flaw you recognize in yourself becomes something you can work to correct. You ought to lay the foundation for what you desire to achieve in your mind at first, and all else will flow into place according to the actions you take to bring to fruition what you've conceived.

Your self-evaluation shouldn't just focus on your weak points. You also want to acknowledge the areas where you're already doing a fantastic job, or where you have already taken steps to improve. When I evaluate myself, I tend to use the "compliment sandwich" model. In this model, you sandwich your constructive criticism between two positive compliments, which act as the bread in the sandwich. This method helps you reinforce all of the positive things you're doing and keeps you motivated to make the necessary changes. At the very least, follow each critical observation with a positive one. For example, you might say, "I'm not *where* I want to be with this skill as yet; nonetheless, I've made a lot of improvement since I started practicing it." Remind yourself of the effort you're making to grow, and positive results will follow. This process may sound like a lot of mental work. After all, it takes significant effort to remain positive and to see this vibe through.

BE HONEST

Finally, one of the most important things to remember when performing a self-evaluation is to be honest. Misrepresenting yourself won't help you improve. You need to work from a fair and accurate picture of yourself, which means you need to avoid being too lenient or too harsh. You don't want to fall into the trap of constantly being critical or even berating yourself for your shortcomings. The desire for improvement is natural, but it should never come from a place of self-loathing. If you look at yourself and all you can see are your negative aspects, you're turning a blind eye to all of your strengths. This can make it incredibly difficult to motivate yourself to make any changes as you start to believe that you will always be lacking in some way. Resist this urge and take a more honest, logical look at yourself. You are sure to find aspects of yourself that you like and some that support your goals too.

At the same time, don't let yourself get away with behaviors you know are bad either. If you know something is holding you back, don't write it off or decide "it's okay for now." While you can't immediately change all of your habits, as they take a while to break, these bad habits will only persist if you don't address them honestly.

Do your best to evaluate yourself honestly. You're never going to be completely objective, but you can try to be as honest as possible. This gives you a rigid foundation from which you can figure out where you need to direct your self-investment efforts. The prospectus you create from this process will enable you to feel confident in your goals and desires and your ability to achieve them.

3

SELF-REGULATION
VALUING SELF-INVESTMENT "ASSETS" AND "COLLATERALS"

When you invest in yourself, your energy is your collateral. It is both the asset you invest and the motivation for not defaulting on your promise to yourself.

What do you think your most significant asset is? This might feel more like the start of a job interview than a legitimate question, but try to consider your answer for a moment. What quality allows you to accomplish more than anything else? In the field of banking, the term asset typically refers to money. More specifically, it refers to a resource that provides value for a person or business, but it is commonly used to talk about value in the form of financial gains. The greater a company's assets, the more the company is worth. This is one way to look at the term, but it is a more narrow view compared to what most people use. An asset has become a term that describes anything useful or valuable.

This could mean it helps you make money, or it could mean it enables you to achieve a particular non-financial goal.

If you broaden your view of the term asset this way, how does this change your answer?

Maybe your gut reaction was to say that your money is your greatest asset. But is that really true? After all, you can generate more money, but you can lose money too if you're not careful. It helps with many issues, yet it can't help with all of them. People with all the money in the world can still start businesses that fail as quickly as they open their doors. The wealthiest people cannot throw money at a guitar and suddenly learn how to play it. Neither can they pay for a tutor and immediately increase their grades without putting in any effort on their part. They cannot buy their way into success without acquiring it through their efforts. Money is useful, but at a certain point, all the money in the world won't help you achieve your goals on its own.

You better work!

If money isn't your greatest asset, then what is?

The one thing that will help you accomplish your goals and get you further in life than anything else is not money, but energy. Energy exertion is a valuable and powerful resource; however, you can only use it effectively in moderation. Hence, the importance of implementing self-regulation in your daily routine.

> *"Many people fail in life, not for lack of ability or brains or even courage but simply because they have never organized their energies around a goal."*
>
> — *ELBERT HUBBARD*

Self-regulation, in and of itself, denotes control of oneself. This practice is essential in executing personal energy management. In this regard, you must regulate your energy with intentions to benefit your pursuit of a better future. The amount of energy you exert when you think, speak, or act ought to be regulated. As individuals who deliberately desire to achieve more as we continue to exist, we need to monitor the volume of energy we employ on specific behaviors. So, once actions are projected to positively affect your future self, it becomes necessary to increase your energy exertion to take full advantage of the value of this action. Don't imprudently employ too much energy in every situation; there are times when little energy is needed to accomplish a task. If you consciously practice self-regulation, you will experience a decrease in impulsiveness and regain control over the amount of energy you apply to each of your behaviors. Consider this practice as a personal value with the willpower to piece your future together in your best interest.

The challenge with this practice lies in one's ability to discover their energy. Some people are not able to tap into their powers to regulate it. These people end up lacking energy, and they rarely start to go after their goals. When they do decide to pursue their goals, they often find it hard to see this mission through to the end, especially if positive results are not immediately apparent. As their limited amount of energy runs out, their progress slows to a crawl and finally comes to a stop. If obstacles appear in their path, they only give up sooner. Without energy, there is no driving force behind your push for success; therefore, there will be no success. You need to discover and refresh yourself daily with a high energy reserve to meet and conquer the challenges that may come your way. Shift your mindset from having a lack of energy to do, to one that envisages an influx of energy.

The energy I've discovered within, and continue to regulate, has enabled me to accomplish so many amazing things. It has transported me above and beyond my expectations, and it ensures that I don't give up when things get tough. It has been the drive that has kept me moving even when everyone else has labeled a task as too difficult. Best of all, energy is a renewable resource. When I find myself running low, I usually rest up and rejuvenate so that later on, I can feel more energetic than ever. Even so, I distance myself from energy drainers—those people and tasks that have left me feeling exhausted in the past. I encourage you to do the same. Though you can expend your energy, you can always get more relatively quickly as long as you don't completely exhaust yourself, as this can compromise your wellness.

If energy is your greatest asset, then it is also your greatest collateral. A collateral is "an asset that a lender accepts as security for a loan" (Kagan, 2020a, para. 1). If someone fails to repay their loan, also known as defaulting on the loan, the collateral is taken in exchange. If you take out a loan to pay for a new car, you might put the car itself up as your collateral. If you make your loan payments on time, you get to keep your vehicle. If not, it gets repossessed, accounting for the remainder of the debt you failed to pay. Similarly, when you invest in yourself, your energy is your collateral.

From the COVID-19 pandemic to a knotty academic affair with my university—The University of the West Indies (UWI), Mona—the year 2020 portrayed behaviors of a delinquent child in need of rehabilitation. The issue I had with the university was vis-à-vis billing logistics. To have been granted permission to submit my Master of Arts (MA) research paper for examination, I had to have paid all outstanding fees. My tuition, accommodation, miscellaneous, and other service fees were paid. In full. I submitted my research on December 20, 2018. On March 23, 2020, my paper had completed its rounds of examination; yet, I could not view my grade due to a financial hold on my student portal.

How can there be a financial hold on my account when I paid all outstanding balances before submitting my research?

I did not quite comprehend why any student who awaits a final research paper grade from an institution—one who has paid the necessary monies to ensure there are no late penalties incurred— would be charged additional fees. This predicament puzzled me.

The UWI, Mona, withheld the award of my MA degree. I contacted several leaders and administrative personnel at the institution, and no one seemed to care very much about my distress. The university's admin informed me that all graduate students must register annually until their examination has been officially declared, and pay appropriate fees. Essentially, if my research underwent examination for three years, I would be required to pay for each of those years.

Rubbish!

I was furious.

I had a lawyer intervene in the matter, which prolonged my case for four months. In August, I thought to myself: "My brain, body muscles, and heart sacrificed a significant amount of energy to complete the MA degree. Why not pay the money and move on to accomplish the string of goals I have laid out for myself?" This moment of introspection led me to pay the outstanding balance that the university arbitrarily placed on my account. It was no small change.

I do not count this as a battle lost. I won! I made a promise to myself that I would complete my master's degree, no matter what. This dilemma was the "no matter what" in the way of me accomplishing this goal. I interrogated the situation and realized that my energy was both the asset I invested and the motivation for not defaulting on such a promise to myself. I regulated and placed a significant portion of energy on the line, spending it in service of my goal to be awarded an MA degree.

You may encounter similar situations. If you give up on your goals, you lose the energy you invested in yourself without any reward. No way was I going to let my energy go to waste. Seeing your self-investment through will allow you to enjoy the rewards at no additional cost. You might even increase your overall energy level, as the thrill of success is very motivating. You may end up with less energy overall, as you feel like your efforts have been wasted. This can leave you feeling unmotivated. When you invest in yourself, you don't want to lose your collateral and let your efforts go to waste, so you are encouraged to keep pushing until you succeed. By wagering your energy, you simultaneously take advantage of your greatest asset and hold yourself accountable for your success.

WHY ENERGY IS YOUR GREATEST ASSET

Energy will get you further than just about any other resource at your disposal. Think about how easy it is to run out of other assets or how ineffective they are in many challenging situations. We already looked at why money isn't as reliable as some people believe. What about assets like time, the number of people you know, or experience? Each of these assets can be helpful in the right circumstance, but none of them can carry the weight of making progress toward your goals on their own.

Let's start by taking a look at time. You should do your best to work efficiently daily, so you make the most of your time because it isn't something you can replace once it has passed. Yes, time is finite, and even if you had an endless amount of time, you still might not be able to get work done without passion. If you've ever tried to write something and simply stared at a blank page for hours, or knowingly procrastinated work because you didn't have the energy to get started on it, or to finish it, then you know that time alone isn't enough to yield success.

> *"A task left undone remains undone in two places—at the actual location of the task, and inside your head. Incomplete tasks in your head consume the energy of your attention as they gnaw at your conscience."*
>
> — BRAHMA KUMARIS

Another common asset that many people prioritize is networking. Certainly, expanding your social circle can help you get noticed and open up new opportunities for you, but what benefit does this offer you if you can't follow through on those opportunities? If a friend of a friend gives you a once-in-a-lifetime opportunity and you let it go to waste because you lack energy, your reputation will suffer. At that point, it won't matter how many people you know, as everyone will be wary about trusting you again.

Finally, let's look at experience. Getting experience in areas relevant to your goals is definitely a critical part of expanding your skillset. The more experience you get, the more confident and comfortable you will be as you continue to pursue your goals. But what happens when you need to do something you've never done before? At a certain point, if you want to continue to develop your skills, you will need to branch out and try new things. You might falter in the absence of experience, especially if you lack the energy necessary to start improving your skills and building experience in new areas.

The issues with relying on all three of these assets have one thing in common. When those assets run out, or when they are not enough to accomplish your goals, you need to fall back on your drive to improve. Each of the above scenarios can be resolved with energy. This is what makes energy your greatest asset. It is something you can use in just about every situation to improve the outcome. You can always rely on energy, and the enthusiasm and motivation it provides you with, to get the results you want to see.

What drives you to improve in one area over another? You might have people in your life who encourage you to improve or other outside factors, but what others want you to do can only go so far toward motivating you. When you hit a wall in your progress, if your enthusiasm and motivation boil down to "someone else wants me to do it," you're going to have a hard time convincing yourself to keep putting in the effort. A much more robust form of conviction and motivation comes from your desire to fulfill your wants and needs. When you genuinely care about what you're trying to do, finding the willpower to stick with it isn't hard at all. This internal motivation is incredibly powerful, and it is all fueled by your most valuable asset—your energy.

Energy is a fantastic motivator! It gets you up and moving, and it helps you shake off the lethargy. When you're energized, you're ready to tackle your goals, no matter how tough the path ahead may seem. So long as you are passionate and enthusiastic about what you are doing, you won't run out of your most valuable asset anytime soon.

ENERGY CAN BE REPLENISHED

Many other resources in our lives are finite. We can't give ourselves more time after personal deadlines have passed. Once time runs out, whether we've put it to good use or not, it's gone. Some resources can be replenished, but they require more effort from you to do so. For example, we can make more money, but there isn't an easy and quick way to do this if we're running low on funds. This is how energy differs from other assets, and another reason it is so valuable to your self-improvement efforts.

Replenishing your energy is incredibly easy compared to other resources. All you need to do is take care of yourself, and your energy will replenish when you take breaks between work or each night as you sleep. Taking care of yourself includes addressing your physical and mental needs. It means practicing proper nutrition, maintaining a consistent sleep schedule, getting some exercise every day, and taking breaks when you start to feel overworked. If you practice all of these things, you will wake up each morning ready to take on whatever the day has in store for you. You will be at maximum energy, and you can contribute all of this energy to additional efforts geared toward self-upliftment.

HOW COLLATERAL MOTIVATES YOU TO SUCCEED

Collateral might sound less than ideal at first. When your investment comes with collateral, you risk losing something if your investment doesn't turn out to be a success. For self-investment, you essentially bet the energy you expend on improving yourself. This risk might initially worry you, but it should only be a problem if you bank on giving up on your goals. If you have every intention of seeing your self-improvement through until you get results, whatever you invest as collateral simply provides extra motivation for you.

We are more motivated when we believe our actions have consequences. If a task or project has no deadline, we're not likely to care much if we finish it or not. There are no negative repercussions for failing to complete it, and even the promise of what we would gain isn't always enough to motivate us to get to work. Think of how many people grow old and give up on their dreams just because they never got the push they needed to take those dreams seriously. However, when there is something to lose—whether it be energy, connections, experience, or whatever it may be—the pressing need to succeed is much more desirable. We can convince ourselves to get up and get moving on the days when we would rather stay in bed. We can ensure we are always thinking about succeeding because we know we don't want all of our hard work and energy to go to waste. Certainly, we should become more motivated and driven because of the personal value of self-investment collateral.

4

SELF-CONFIDENCE
"DEPOSITING" BELIEF IN YOURSELF

Over time, continual deposits of belief in yourself will add up, and before long, the doubt that once held you back will be a thing of the past.

If you've ever watched a documentary film that covers successful people who are remarkable at their craft prepare for future events, you have definitely been introduced to admirable confidence on display. These people are very persistent in their approach and believe that they will achieve success in all their attempts—they will repetitively be their very best. They know, without a doubt, they will succeed. They also are aware that if they don't, they will learn valuable lessons that will cause them to improve. This is confidence.

Self-confidence and self-esteem go hand in hand. Both terms signify awareness that your abilities can positively impact your future. People with high levels of self-esteem have genuine respect for themselves and confidence in their aptitude. Without self-confidence, you may feel helpless, buffeted by the often-unkind winds of fate. More so, you may believe your efforts will affect your success, but only in the sense that they will make you less likely to succeed. If you activate your self-confidence, it is more likely that you will perform better and achieve success that will further elevate your confidence.

A low self-confidence is a form of self-sabotage. Whenever you look at a new task you've never tried before, the first thought in your head might be something to the effect of, "I can't do this!" You worry that you will mess it up, and you fear that messing one task up will snowball until you have effectively messed your whole life up. Whether these thoughts are rational or not isn't necessary at that moment. All you can think of is the mortifying, often paralyzing fear that stepping out of your comfort zone will only result in embarrassment and catastrophic failure.

When you doubt your abilities, it becomes tough to put yourself in a position to take risks. The fear of failure begins to overpower the prospect of even the most promising possible rewards until you are too afraid to try something new. Doubt is incredibly powerful, and it can keep you from trying things you might otherwise excel at, given enough time to practice and develop your skills. Unfortunately, the road to success often involves many different risks. If you want to get into a competitive university, you need to apply and risk being denied. If you're going to ask someone out on a date, you need to risk the possibility that they won't accept it. If you desire to learn a new skill, you need to start at a beginner level and surrender that your initial attempts are not going to be as incredible as an expert's. If you are not confident enough to take risks because you're too worried about failure, you won't be able to reap the rewards of success because you haven't given yourself a chance to succeed.

Nourishing your self-esteem is like making deposits into your bank account. The more you deposit, the more you will save, and the more interest you will make on your self-confidence levels. Having high self-esteem is critical to paving the path to success. It will help you push back against doubt and worry that could otherwise interfere with your self-investment. With high confidence, you will start to appreciate and even anticipate opportunities to learn something new. These opportunities are no longer chances to fail, but rather chances to succeed. Therefore, you want to make as many deposits of self-esteem into your mindset as you possibly can. Over time, continual deposits of belief in yourself will add up, and before long, the doubt that once held you back will be a thing of the past.

Each day I live has taught me a new lesson about the very imbrication between life and one's self. These lessons have taught me how to actualize self-assurance and have guided me on a path that brought my full self to life. I use the terminology "full self" to paint a vivid picture of a container filled with something good. Prior to this discovery, the level of assurance I needed to function as a champion without reservation was inadequate; *self* was nowhere near full. It is from these lack of self-confidence narratives I eventually conquered, that I make sense of the person I am today.

In 2012, I entered the Schools' Science and Technology Societies oratory competition hosted by the Scientific Research Council (SRC).

The competition's format required that I submit a copy of my speech for screening against a score sheet that graded for relevance, facts, conclusiveness, purpose, ability to persuade, and use of language. A preview of each competitor's speech allowed the judges to select the best ones to advance to the finals. I worked extremely hard to write a good enough speech on the assigned topic. When I received my scores back, they appeared in a table format, with the winner's scores brandished next to mine, for comparison purposes—I suppose.

My score was 42.8, and the winner had a 42.9. *You're a failure by point one,* I told myself. Having the winner's score next to mine didn't do me any good. I instantly began to question my capability to deliver my speech in the final round. *Can I...? Must I...? Will I...?* Quite honestly, though my score was short a few points from being displayed ostentatiously in the winner's column, dusky fumes of failure headed my direction.

What if I stumble on my syllables?

What if, after I present my speech, I end up with the lowest overall score in the competition?

It was never—*what if I win?*

I remember expressing the slightest feeling of defeat to Ms. Thomas—one of my science teachers in high school—and she reminded me of my oratory competence and motivated me to improve on it for the competition.

The overpowering thoughts of failure that once flooded my mind experienced drought. I began to believe in my ability to speak well.

Day after day, leading up to the finale of the oratory competition, I did my very best to let confidence flow through the channels of my mindset. I repeated authentic affirmations of victory every time I looked at my speech, and I believed every ounce of what I said. The doubt and worry that were lurking in my mind to rob me of a victory were deceased. On competition day, I spoke to captivate, clarify, and convince. At that moment, I knew I had done my best. For my hours of preparation and my self-belief, the SRC awarded me as the 2012 champion orator.

Remember that self-investment is a risk of its own that requires you to have some faith in yourself. However, when you get past the initial fear of investing, you realize that self-investment has a very low risk of ending poorly for you and a very high chance of reward. Like many other risks you may need to take, it is not nearly as frightening as you might initially make it out to be in your head. If you can deposit enough belief in yourself to overcome your fear of investing in yourself, you can do the same for other sources of doubt. When you begin believing in yourself and become willing to try new things and see how they go, you will notice that many of the horrible consequences you imagined only existed in your head. Let go of doubt, and you will never let an opportunity to make progress on your goals pass you by again.

"Doubt kills more dreams than failure ever will."

— *SUZY KASSEM*

WHY LOW SELF-CONFIDENCE OCCURS

You've probably known people who seem to exude confidence everywhere they go. They have no problem volunteering themselves for new opportunities and experiences. These kinds of people often strike up conversations with strangers, and they rarely feel stage fright. It seems like there is very little they wouldn't do. They are not held back by doubt and worry, so they can try just about anything, and more often than not, it seems to work out for them. I am one such person who feels confident in new situations and desires to try new things. My confidence enables me to achieve more than I would if I couldn't recognize my self-worth. Though I see myself as a confident person, I too, need a confidence boost now and again.

If you struggle with low self-esteem, you might wonder how I, and others like me, can be so self-confident all the time. Of course, confident people weren't born that way, just like you weren't born with a lack of confidence. Your self-esteem developed over time due to your experiences and your disposition, just as theirs did. You can learn to be self-confident too, but first, you must examine why self-confidence eludes you, to start changing your mindset and appreciating your self-worth.

To improve your confidence, you first need to understand why you lack self-confidence. By getting to the root of the problem, you can begin to turn around the self-defeating mindset you have built up by nourishing your self-esteem instead. Several different factors can contribute to low self-esteem. Sometimes this fear manifests itself from a particularly bad, sometimes even traumatic, experience with failure. Other times, it may be the result of many small incidents that, over the years, built up and convinced you that you weren't as capable or successful as your peers. Identifying the reason for your own difficulties with self-esteem allows you to take a more practical approach toward becoming a more confident person.

PAST EXPERIENCES

If we are taught to believe that we won't be successful, it becomes difficult to believe in ourselves. Negative past experiences can create doubts in our minds that undermine our self-esteem. Sometimes, these are memories of times where we tried our hardest to achieve something and fell short. This failure can sting, and if we let ourselves feel bad about our lack of success for too long, we can start to internalize the idea that we won't succeed at anything else either. Another possible cause of low self-esteem is past traumatic events. These can interfere with our sense of self-worth.

If you have experienced the pain of failure before, you know it's not always easy to convince yourself to give things another try. Your immediate reaction might be to avoid any situation you're not entirely comfortable with. This is no way to live your life. If you reject all new experiences that come your way and only stick to what you know, you won't be able to invest in yourself and improve. In order to benefit from self-investment, you must convince yourself that your past experiences of failure don't define your chances of future success.

THE WRONG MINDSET

If you want to improve your life, having the right mindset is everything. Without a positive, long-term mindset that encourages you to work hard to achieve your goals, you might give up before you ever see the results of your efforts. A proper attitude gives you the motivation to achieve your goals. However, sometimes otherwise-helpful mindsets can emphasize the results and not enough on the process that led to those results. If you expect immediate change from yourself and you don't allow yourself the time you need to grow and learn new things, you're only going to be frustrated when you don't see those changes as quickly as you want. If you strive for perfection, especially when you are only just starting out learning a new skill or idea, you're only going to burden yourself with unnecessary stress.

A perfectionist mindset can sink your confidence levels faster than almost anything else. After all, none of us are perfect. If you hold yourself to the standard of perfection every time you try something, you're going to fall short, and you will treat this result as a failure instead of just one step on the path to success. You might leap immediately to blaming yourself rather than recognizing that you need to give yourself time to improve. This injures your confidence and makes you less likely to try again, keeping you from getting the experience you need to see better results. This isn't to say that you shouldn't expect greatness from yourself. Setting a high bar gives you something to aim for, but your bar shouldn't be set so high that it's completely unrealistic. Otherwise, you will only lower your self-confidence with every attempted task—rather than raise it.

The perfectionist mindset deals in black and white logic! If you are not perfect at a task, you have completely failed at it. However, when you take a more realistic approach to your development, you start to see that the truth of the matter isn't nearly as clear-cut. Maybe you didn't completely achieve what you set out to do, but you still got some practice in. This practice improved your skills and taught you what to do and what not to do next time. This is valuable information, perhaps even more valuable than if you had gotten lucky and succeeded on your first try. You can incorporate this information into your next attempt, getting better and better every time at whatever skill you're trying to improve. With each improved result, you deposit a little more belief into yourself, raising your self-esteem. Instead of seeing each attempt as failing, you start to see those attempts as an improvement over the last. This is a much healthier mindset, and it will help you achieve a lot more than perfectionism ever will.

MAKING COMPARISONS

One of the worst things we do for our self-confidence is compare ourselves to other people. We look at what others have, whether we're looking at leaders in our fields or we're just endlessly scrolling through social media. Others may have the fame and fortune that we desire. They might post a perfect photo of their family or a vacation they took on social media, garnering hundreds of likes and dozens of comments. After a while, we start to wonder why we don't have the same things in our lives. Jealousy and frustration rear their ugly heads. Instead of feeling encouraged to take action and start achieving all of these things for ourselves, we often become jaded and dejected. We insist that we will never be as successful as they are, and we start giving up on our self-improvement investments before we have allowed the account to mature.

One thing we often forget when we're looking at the accomplishments of others, so proudly shared across the web, is that we're seeing what they want us to see. Social media profiles are perfectly curated to reflect extraordinary lives. After all, would you post about the messy argument you had with your family, or would you post a smiling, happy picture of all of you? Would you be more likely to post a picture of you at work or the unforgettable vacation you took, even though you spend far more time at work? With social media, we see what others want us to see. Rarely is it an accurate reflection of anyone else's life. This means that when our immediate reactions to seeing these kinds of posts are something along the lines of, "Why do they have this fantastic life and I don't?" or "Why are they successful and I'm not?" we should try to remember that this is only a small slice of their lives. They may be experiencing the same daily hardships we are, and they likely had to work hard and invest in themselves for a long time before they achieved half the things they post about.

When we focus so much on what others are doing, we fail to focus on ourselves. We stop investing in ourselves, only growing more envious of what others have achieved without giving ourselves the tools to achieve the same level of success. It is better to be concerned with what we are doing than spend most of our time worrying about others. When we focus on our development and accept that we will grow at our own pace, we will abandon the need to look for validation by comparing ourselves to others. This leaves us feeling more capable and confident in ourselves.

HOW TO START BELIEVING IN YOURSELF

Cultivating self-confidence is a crucial component of self-investment. When you start depositing belief in yourself, you gain a greater appreciation for your abilities and skills. You start noticing your improvement every day, even if it's just by a small amount. It also becomes easier to expand your skills, as you start viewing every time you try something new as an opportunity to learn. More so, your confidence grows, feeding back into your sense of self-efficacy, and you start trusting yourself so much so that investing in yourself no longer feels like the big risk it once was.

There are many different therapeutic strategies that I use to improve my self-esteem. Mindfulness, cognitive behavioral therapy, and exposure therapy have all been used to help people develop confidence and manage fears. We'll look at some of the behaviors and theories that make up these therapeutic strategies. You can incorporate these practices and mindset adjustments into your daily life to elevate your confidence and reveal the smart, capable person you really are.

CONFRONT AND REFRAME NEGATIVE THOUGHTS

I am convinced that the greatest obstacle many people face in their lifetime is their imperfect perception of themselves. The vast majority of your negative thoughts about yourself are not logical. Low self-esteem causes your mind to twist the truth or exaggerate it until you can find a way to blame yourself for bad things and relinquish the credit for good things. If you learn to recognize these overly critical thoughts when they appear and start thinking logically about them, you can disprove many of the lies you tell yourself when you struggle with your self-esteem. This process is used in the cognitive behavioral therapy method.

The method suggests that every time you think something uncharitable about yourself, you should pause, evaluate the falsity of the thought, and then try to replace it with something closer to the truth. For example, say you had to take an exam in a class, and you did poorly. Your first thought might be something like, "I did terribly because I'm not smart enough to do better. I'm a failure." But is this statement really true? The issue does not lie in being smart enough to do well. The problem lies in the amount of energy you are willing to invest in doing well on the next test. Identify that the thought is unhelpful and untrue, and then try to choose something that comes closer to the truth, instead. For example, you might replace the thought with, "I didn't do well this time, but that's because I didn't give it my all. Next time I will study a little harder, and I will do better," or, "I didn't get the grade I wanted because I didn't understand this concept. I will ask someone to explain it to me so I can do better next time." These thoughts, and others that are similar, come with the implicit assumption that you can and will improve as long as you take the necessary steps. They avoid the defeatist attitude that would otherwise lead you to believe that additional effort is pointless. They shift the blame away from things you cannot change toward the things you have control over. This is a very empowering feeling.

Over time, you will start to notice when you're thinking poorly about yourself for no reason. You will begin picking up on all the small, reactionary thoughts you have about yourself, and you will start replacing them with more logical thoughts. When you stop beating yourself up all the time, you allow yourself to see your good qualities too. Through this process, you will acquire more agency and motivation to improve along with your newfound confidence. No longer will you be sabotaged by your inner saboteur.

ACCEPT YOUR EMOTIONS

Denial is a potent force, especially when you deny your emotional response to a situation. When you are stuck in denial about what you're feeling, you tend to sweep your feelings under the rug, but they don't actually go away. You might feel hurt and upset when things go wrong, but you tell yourself that you need to remain positive at all times or that being very upset is weak. Forcing your emotions down like this isn't healthy. It's good to maintain an optimistic attitude, but being optimistic doesn't mean you can never be sad or frustrated. These feelings are a natural part of life, and lying to yourself about your emotions or blaming yourself for having them in the first place only encourages you to heap more criticism on yourself. If you tell yourself you're not allowed to be upset, then every time you are upset becomes a personal failure.

Emotional acceptance is a key step in mindfulness. Feeling and expressing your emotions is far better than ignoring them or disparaging yourself for having them. Positivity is good, but you must also leave space for other feelings. You will have good days and bad days, and it doesn't help to punish yourself for the bad days. Allow yourself to experience the uglier emotions. This lets you get them out of your system so you can start the next day from a place and mental space of peace. Furthermore, when you encourage yourself to be honest about your feelings, you will also find it easier to express positive emotions like joy and pride.

SEEK OUT NEW EXPERIENCES

Avoiding something that scares us only makes it more frightening. If your low self-esteem is connected to a particular task or behavior that gives you anxiety, or if you shy away from trying new things because you fear failing, you make the fear much more prominent in your mind. You may start to think unrealistically about whatever it is you're afraid of, building it up to be a more negative experience than it really is. Let's say you want to start a new hobby, but you're worried you won't be any good at it. You tell yourself you're not good enough—so, why even try? If you mess up, you could completely embarrass yourself. Everyone would laugh at you, and you would only feel worse about yourself. As a result, you avoid trying the new hobby altogether. But are the consequences you made up in your head really accurate? Do you think everyone would laugh at you if you weren't immediately perfect at something you'd never done before? Maybe not. But it's hard to convince yourself of this if you don't have any prior experience you can use as evidence.

"Always be ready to attack those feelings of 'not good enough' with a reminder of who you are or who you plan to become. Be pulled into action by the clarity of knowing thyself" (Tomlinson, 2018, p. 41).

When you start trying new things and taking chances, you see that things work out in your favor more often than you might think. This isn't to say you will immediately become an expert; however, you probably won't experience the harsh criticism you were worried about, which kept you from trying in the first place. Instead, you will most likely see others offering their support. You will find that the things you were dreading for so long are not so scary after all, which empowers you to keep trying and pushing yourself, none of which would have been possible if you let your low self-esteem get in your way. This is a form of exposure therapy. The more frequently you take risks, starting with small things and working your way up to more significant investments, the more confidence you will have in yourself, and the less fear you will feel toward the investments you make. All of this helps you live a life free of self-doubt. As you continue to deposit belief in yourself, your self-confidence will grow, and your abilities will improve. So, whether you've developed confidence which now oozes from your very presence, or you've allowed the onslaught of life's difficulties to rear cunning insecurities in you, it is your responsibility to reinforce your self-confidence.

5

SELF-RELIANCE

YOU ARE THE "BENEFICIARY" OF YOUR SELF-INVESTMENT

As the beneficiary of your self-investment, understanding the many ways you stand to benefit will give you the extra push you need to improve your lot in life until you've actualized a future where success abounds.

In finance, a beneficiary is a person who receives the payouts of a will, life insurance policy, or trust. As the name implies, it is the person who benefits from these investments. In most cases, this person is different from the one who made the initial investment. For example, parents may pay into a life insurance policy, while their child or other dependent may ultimately receive the funds. If someone writes a will, they distribute their possessions and wealth to those they leave behind when they die. However, this is a little different when you are investing in yourself. Instead of paying out benefits to others, all of the profits go to yourself. You become the beneficiary of your self-investment.

But before you can reap the rewards of your investment in yourself, you ought to develop self-reliance, a concept that charges dependence on self rather than others. As I grow older, I recognize that I am continually being socialized in ways that teach me to live independently. However, this independence comes with problem-solving and decision-making responsibilities that cause me to think critically before committing to my actions. These skills enable me to experience and feel comfortable, confident, and courageous in myself—and about myself. As a self-reliant person, I am now fully capable of flourishing as I discover my personal growth and cherish my accomplishments.

Being self-reliant does not mean you should shoulder your hardships alone. If you encounter a roadblock, seek help. Personally, this is something I did quite often. In late August of 2013, I was granted on-campus accommodation on Taylor Hall at my university, at a price I could not afford. My hometown was just shy of an hour-and-a-half drive to the university's campus, in Kingston—one bus ride and one taxi, and in some cases, two bus rides and a taxi. In this instance, I relied heavily on myself to map out a plan that would provide enough funds to cover my accommodation fee. The ideas that came to mind included generating a post on Facebook and disseminating emails to all my contacts requesting financial assistance to cover boarding for semester one.

I spent several hours on my Uncle's desktop computer trying to type the perfect post for Facebook and a compelling enough email. At one point, I thought to myself, *what will others think of my family and me when they read my post or email?* Pride reared its ugly head and convinced me to trash the idea completely. And that I did. I decided I would travel to and from university via public transportation for a while longer. There were days when my lectures ended late in the evening, and I arrived home close to midnight. I will never forget that my grandmother would wait up for me, knowing the *streets* was no place for me to be passed a certain hour—especially in Jamaica.

Question: Have you ever fallen asleep on public transportation and missed your stop?

That was the norm for me on my trips home from university, though I knew it was unsafe. I was too tired after the long lecture and extracurricular activity-filled days, and besides, the sounds and motions of public transportation at night are far more calming than any sleeping pill could ever be. Truth be told, my body was worn out, and the little money I had for meals and transportation was insufficient. Though I was fearful of what my peers would think of me and my life, I swallowed my pride and reverted to the initial idea I had.

Click! My post was uploaded on Facebook.

Click! Click! Click! I sent several emails.

This idea was successfully executed, and the response was overwhelming. Money poured into my bank account, in abundance, so much so that I could pay a significant portion of the accommodation fee for the following semester also. I am forever grateful to everyone who contributed. Every dollar helped, in some way or another, to fund a portion of my university expenses. Separate and apart from financial contributions, people were very supportive. My Facebook post got numerous likes and comments, and was shared by many, and I received several congratulatory email replies filled with words of encouragement. A young lady by the name of Rasheida who attended Broward College in Florida, wrote me saying:

"First, let me say congrats on your achievement. I am a college student myself and I know how hard it is coming from a middle-class background... This week is a [bit] slow for me because it's rent week. I know in my heart that my money won't go to waste, so next week I will send you $30 US. Good luck."

Asking for help does not weaken your strength; it only recharges your energy to accomplish what you are destined to achieve. Show yourself a little kindness and compassion from time to time. After all, who better to rely on and gain love and sympathy from but yourself? Happiness abounds when a person bravely journeys toward their goals and obtains the fresh fruits of their labor along the way.

As the beneficiary of your self-investment efforts, you receive all of the rewards of your hard work. Your self-improvement may improve the lives of others too, but only because you are helping yourself first. You are working toward achieving your own dreams, not the dreams of others. Your goals should always be tailored to help you complete tasks that appeal to you and bring you closer to the kind of life you want to lead. By focusing on yourself before you worry about others, you ensure that everyone benefits—this is the power of self-reliance.

Some peoples' lives are entirely defined by the expectations others have of them. They might pursue a particular career because their parents want them to make a lot of money, or they might change their future plans to fit a romantic partner's intentions. It's good to want to help others, but it shouldn't come at the expense of your own happiness and vision of success. If you force yourself to work toward goals you don't care about, you don't actually benefit from succeeding. If, instead, you pursue things you're passionate about, your success will uplift everyone around you. You will be more motivated to follow through on your goals, and you can use your newfound fulfillment and financial freedom to support your loved ones—if that is what you desire.

Personal gain is also a powerful motivator. When you know exactly how you will benefit from self-investment, you will have no problem committing to invest. After all, you know the work you put in will be worth it. As the beneficiary of your self-investment, understanding the many ways you stand to benefit will give you the extra push you need to improve your lot in life until you've actualized a future where success abounds.

THE LIFE-CHANGING POWER OF SELF-INVESTMENT

Self-investment can improve your life in so many ways. It has the power to completely reshape various aspects of your life, which is what makes self-improvement so worthy of investing in. You don't have to worry that you will put in more than you will get out either, as you're never at risk of losing something when you strive to improve yourself. You only stand to gain.

Everything you do should begin with a mindset that desires to see an improvement in yourself. Self-investment opens up your future to hundreds of different possibilities, each one better than the last. From here, you will also see growth in your personal relationships, your financial situation, your ability to make progress toward your goals, and your overall happiness and sense of fulfillment. With all these benefits, sticking with self-investment becomes a no-brainer.

IMPROVING YOURSELF

The primary goal of investing in yourself is to improve yourself. You reap what you sow, and if what you sow is self-investment, then what you will reap is self-improvement. When you develop your skills and fix your mindset, you will be able to accomplish more than you could before. You will find more success in your career and your personal life, and you will develop a growth-oriented mentality that will help you manage even the most difficult of hardships. Self-improvement is an excellent way to get your life in the shape you want it to be. You can become the ultimate version of yourself.

Improving yourself puts you in a better position to improve the lives of others as well. This is why it is so important to focus on yourself before you worry about helping others. If you lack the resources, skills, or money necessary to help someone without hurting yourself, you won't be able to provide them with help for very long. You will both end up barely scraping by, and the money and other resources you had to offer will dwindle as a result. When you help yourself first, you amass enough resources that can allow you to make a significant impact on someone else's life. You may even provide them with the encouragement they need to improve themselves too, which would be a wonderful gift. The more you improve yourself, the better off you are to improve other areas of your life and the lives of your friends, family, and community.

REDUCING RESISTANCE

You will face many obstacles on your road to success. You may experience temporary setbacks, or you may encounter problems so drastic that they seem to derail your life plans altogether. These challenges can make you feel as though you've come to the end of the road, especially if you lack the skills needed to navigate your way past them. But when you invest in yourself by developing your abilities and cultivating determination and critical thinking skills, these challenges are not nearly as enormous as they once appeared. In fact, you may be able to address them relatively quickly and be back on the path to success sooner than you think. There will be very little resistance holding you back from your goals after all.

Resistance comes in many different forms. A difficult exam or having a tough time at work are problems, but so are having a buildup of stress in your life, carrying around tension, being at odds with your emotions, and similar issues. Investing in yourself can help you deal with these kinds of resistance too. When you improve your self-reliance, it's easier to find a work-life balance that works for you. You still want to push yourself, but you also start to recognize that self-care is important too. When you feel more in tune with your emotions, it becomes easier to express them and alleviate tension and doubt. As you improve your life circumstances, you will be able to find more time for relaxation while still being motivated and focused enough to complete any work you need to get done. As you continue to benefit from self-investment, these mental and emotional forms of resistance will melt away.

IMPROVING YOUR RELATIONSHIPS

It's hard to maintain a healthy relationship with someone else when you are so wrapped up in your personal issues. If you struggle with insecurity, doubt, and a lack of success in your career, these problems can leach into your relationships and make them more challenging to maintain. When you invest in yourself, you reduce the likelihood of this happening because you eliminate many things that would otherwise strain your relationships. The more you improve, the easier it will be to form and maintain long-lasting relationships.

Additionally, self-investment provides you with tools that can help you manage conflicts and find common ground in relationships. For example, if you work on being honest with yourself and expressing how you feel, you also become more comfortable being honest with others. Improving your communication skills helps you get your point across more clearly, and these skills can also help you form new relationships. You build the confidence you need to start conversations with people you don't already know, which is as relevant for business networking as it is for building personal relationships. Your social circle will expand, and the links you already have will become closer than ever before. With plenty of friends and family by your side, achieving success is all the more worthwhile.

MAKING HEADWAY ON YOUR GOALS

Having a dream for your future is one thing, but making headway toward achieving that dream is another thing entirely. Many people have dreams, but very few people make the self-investment required to follow through on the promises they make to themselves. When you invest in yourself, you should always keep your goals in mind, as this is one area where you are likely to benefit the most. Part of the reason is that by developing your skills and abilities, you are becoming more capable and more prepared for the challenges life throws your way. Another part of the reason is that you are motivating yourself more efficiently than ever before. Focus and drive, two traits that may have previously been in short supply, are now readily abundant because you are working toward goals that matter to you. When you care about the progress you're making, and you can see how your investments are already improving your life, you will find it easier to continue pushing forward until you successfully achieve your goals.

As you continue making progress on your goals, you may also find that you're acquiring a greater sense of clarity regarding what you want to do with your life. If you are still young, you don't have to have your whole life planned out already. If you are older, you already know that becoming an adult does not necessarily mean you know what direction you want to take in life, nor does it mean you have to pick a single path and stick with it forever. When you seek new experiences in your quest to improve yourself, you start to get a feel for what you enjoy and what brings you stress. This can help you obtain a future career path or get another life goal into focus. As you keep scoring goals of accomplishment, you can shift your goalpost further and further toward new dreams you discover along the way. This ensures you are always working toward the next great thing in your life, as you follow through with plans of enriching your self-investment account with purpose and determination.

CREATING NEW OPPORTUNITIES FOR GROWTH

Achieving the original goal you had in mind when you started investing in yourself isn't the end of the road. You can certainly take time to celebrate your success and be proud of yourself for what you have accomplished—as you should. However, you should also start thinking about what comes next for you. When investors sell their stocks and make a hefty profit, does it make more sense for them to rest on their heels, slowly letting the money they've earned dwindle to nothing, or should they reinvest the money and double or triple their earning potential? Those who have earned the most from the stock market know they should always be looking for the next opportunity to reinvest. Similarly, you can reinvest in yourself and build upon the personal and professional success you've already achieved—to end up accomplishing even greater things.

As your self-investment efforts begin to pay off and you accomplish bigger and better things, more opportunities will appear. Someone might take notice of your hard work and offer you a spot on their next big project. A friend of a friend you met through networking yourself might see your potential and present you with a chance to show off your skills or develop them further. These new opportunities will help you set new and much better goals as you surpass your old ones. They will give you a chance to continue investing in yourself and improving until you are living your dream life.

How I managed to complete university debt-free was nothing short of a miracle, yes, but it was more so a reward for prior self-upliftment investments. Sometime in February of 2013, the UWI, Mona, offered me a place as a full-time student to read for a Bachelor of Arts degree majoring in Entertainment and Cultural Enterprise Management. I was expected to indicate my acceptance within five months' time. July was fast approaching, and I knew not how I would cover the cost of my tuition. I was raised in a single-parent household, and my father never worked the kind of job that could accumulate enough money over time to send me off to university without worry. Though the struggle was real—as millennials would say—I took a leap of faith and accepted the offer. This bold decision increased my drive to find a way to enter and exit the gates of the UWI, Mona, avoiding hitting a financial rock bottom of deep student loan debts.

Though my search for tertiary education scholarships began later than the typical university student, I was able to locate and apply for quite a few. My mindset believed every word in a Jamaican proverb my grandmother introduced to me at a young age—"every mickle make a muckle." The proverb simply means every small thing can add up to something far greater. I remember telling myself that if I applied for several smaller scholarships and was awarded a few, they could add up and cover a considerable portion of my tuition.

August came really quick that year. It was almost time for the school semester to officially begin. I had saved a few dollars. The only thing it could pay for was transportation to and from the university's campus for a few days. When I finally realized that I had insufficient funds to attend university, I was lying in bed with my legs propped up on pillows arranged comfortably. At home, I am sure my depression was clear through my facial expressions as I battled with feelings of hopelessness that permeated my chest.

Ping!

My Blackberry phone received a text message.

It was Ms. Thomas, the science teacher I mentioned earlier, asking me for permission to call. On the call, she expressed that a gentleman at a prominent entertainment company in the United States—who wished to remain unknown—reached out to her because he had been continuously impressed with my progress and wanted to cover the cost of my tertiary education. I could not believe a word she was saying because I was in shock.

How did this man know about me?

I couldn't tell you. What I do know is that he spotted potential in me. All the self-investment decisions I made in secondary school led to this ecstatic, yet unbelievable, moment. Knowing that my academic and social investments enthused someone and that they wanted to invest in my development further made me focus on investing even more in myself to consciously and continuously make everyone who was rooting for me proud.

The process of self-investment may start slow, but as you begin to see returns on your investments, these returns will grow exponentially bigger over time. As the beneficiary of your self-investment, every new opportunity and goal you set is another chance to grow, as well as to experience the benefits that come with this growth. Your narrative may not be the same as mine. But do know that the small investments you make in yourself will eventually develop into astonishing results that allow you to live the way you want to. In short, self-investment can help you transform your life.

II

WITHDRAWING TRIUMPH

6

SELF-DETERMINATION
ACQUIRING DEVELOPMENTAL "DIVIDENDS"

Shifting your focus from the distant future by identifying developmental dividends on your self-investment journey will motivate you to persevere.

Investing in the stock market inherently requires you to take on a certain level of risk. You can't be absolutely certain that you're going to see the kind of returns you'd like. Not everyone who invests in stocks becomes a millionaire, and some may lose money instead. This can make the idea of investing intimidating for a novice, as they may feel anxious about risking their money, knowing they may not get all of it back. You might feel similar anxiety regarding self-investment. What if you spend all of your time improving your skills and making yourself a better person, and you still fall short of your dream life? Was all of your effort wasted?

When you're improving yourself, no effort is really wasted. Even if you do not achieve your initial goals, you still have an opportunity to reap significant rewards from your efforts. Additionally, you don't have to wait years to see if your self-investment pays off. You can see the change right in front of your eyes in the form of developmental dividends.

Some stocks offer dividends for their shareholders. A dividend is "the distribution of some of a company's earnings to a class of its shareholders" (Chen, 2020, para. 1), and it usually is determined by the growth of the stock over time. Dividends help you mitigate your risk by guaranteeing small returns on your investments over time. They are sums of money paid regularly—typically quarterly—out of a company's profits or reserves. When companies offer dividends, they are trying to assure shareholders that their stocks are still profitable. They are smaller payments that keep people invested in holding on to their stocks, allowing them to continue to increase in value. Dividends are the "breadcrumbs" that keep investors attentive to their investment.

We ought to enforce self-determination to follow the breadcrumbs trail on the road to our success story. Self-determination is a goal-oriented and developmental construct that is rooted in the tenets of motivation and skill enhancement. Once you intentionally decide to enforce this concept to pursue your lifelong goals, you will make conscious decisions that will bring forth developmental dividends. These are the minor accomplishments that will position you to successfully enroll in the school you wish, get a job you are passionate about, or even move up the ranks in your organization. If you are self-determined, you will make things happen in your favor in your life. Focusing your mindset on executing volitional actions will add oxygen to the flames of your motivational truths.

If you worry that your self-investment won't pay off, start looking for dividends. Shifting your focus from the distant future by identifying developmental dividends on your self-investment journey will motivate you to persevere. Change doesn't happen all at once. It occurs in small amounts over time, and you can see the evidence of these more minor changes if you look. Any time you notice yourself addressing a situation differently from how you might have done so before, or when you look back at your past work and see that your skills have significantly improved, you see the developmental dividends of your self-investment. You might not have reached your goals just yet, but taking note of the progress you've already made can give you the motivation you need to keep investing in yourself, knowing it's already paying off.

I made a declaration that I will make every effort to pursue a doctoral degree to get a career in post-secondary education—and that I am determined to achieve. My lifelong goal is to become a lecturer. Daily, I am constantly reminded of and motivated to persevere toward this goal, because of the developmental dividends I've acquired thus far from my efforts. Interestingly, while I was pursuing my MA degree at The University of the West Indies, Mona, I was designated as a writing tutor for undergraduates by the Office of Student Services and Development, Academic Support Unit. Additionally, while pursuing an Associate in Fine Arts in Theater in the US, I was asked to be a student assistant tutor for writing. These experiences have most certainly helped me to fine-tune my teaching skills. I have assisted my Jamaican and American peers and a few international students who have had diverse backgrounds writing specifically for academic purposes.

Both experiences are unmatched, yet each of their value contributes to my progress toward achieving one of my long-term goals. I am invested in accomplishing my dream of becoming a lecturer, to the point where my determination has not only allowed my capability as an efficient instructor to shine through; it also led me to decipher my strengths and limitations in the field. Note carefully, the experiences I have gained helping my peers at different levels of higher education indicate developmental dividends, which can help me pursue a career in post-secondary education. These dividends are deliberately delineated as developmental because they have heightened my teaching skills, knowledge, rapport with others, and my belief in self—all very vital fundamentals on my goal-oriented journey.

TYPES OF DEVELOPMENTAL DIVIDENDS

Developmental dividends come in many forms. Depending on what goals you're trying to achieve and what skills you're building up in the process, you're going to see different kinds of progress. It's essential to recognize all examples of development, even if they're not what you would typically think of when you look for the results of your efforts. Completing tasks on your to-do list is one way to measure the amount of headway you've made since you've started investing in yourself, but it's not the only way. Improving an individual skill can also be a developmental dividend, as can changes in your mentality and relationships. Learning to recognize the smaller milestones on the way to your bigger goals will inspire you to keep going.

MAKING PROGRESS TOWARD YOUR GOALS

Getting closer to your goals is the most definite sign that what you're doing is working. This type of developmental dividend is often the easiest to recognize, especially if you're working to keep your goals in mind at all times. When you make progress toward your goals, you complete tasks and other activities that form the pathway to success. If your goal is to get a better final grade in a class, then the progress toward that goal might include completing homework assignments, studying routinely, and performing well enough on preliminary exams. Each of these smaller tasks is necessary for a more significant result. Embracing self-determination to see these smaller accomplishments through, will bring you one step closer to achieving a better final grade in the class.

Completing tasks makes us feel accomplished, no matter the size or scope of the task at hand. This isn't just speculation—it's backed up by studies of our brains. We have an internal positive feedback system that runs on the release of the brain chemical dopamine. When you "recognize a task or project as completed, your brain releases a load of dopamine, a neurotransmitter that is responsible for generating feelings of accomplishment, satisfaction, and happiness" (Sáez, n.d., para. 2). As a result, you feel great about what you're doing, and you're more likely to repeat the behavior in the future. This is what makes checklists so helpful. You get that spike of dopamine every time you check a task off your to-do list. After a while, these good behaviors become ingrained in your life, turning into daily habits. Remember that our actions are the result of good habits building up over time. Each task you complete may not feel like a lot of effort on its own, but as these good habits stack up, it becomes easy to see all of the progress you have already made.

Even though this is the most self-evident type of developmental dividend, it's still possible to fail to recognize the progress you've made. If you're not improving at the rate you initially hoped for, it's easy to feel like you haven't improved at all, even if this is far from true. When in doubt, remind yourself of all of the small tasks you have already completed, and try to consider their cumulative effect. Think about where you were before you started down this path of progress and reflect on all the work you have already put in since then. You will often find that you've accomplished a lot more than you think.

IMPROVING YOUR SKILLS

Improvement doesn't just come in the form of completing tasks. You can also recognize your progress by assessing the results of all of your practice on your skills. As you continue working toward your goals, you will get better at the abilities relevant to those goals. Continual practice with a paintbrush will make you a better artist, every book you read will make you a better writer, and every deal you weren't able to close will make you a better salesperson. You learn something from each experience, whether that experience ends in success or failure. If you succeed, you know what to do for the future, and you can repeat the process. If you don't quite hit the mark, you learn what not to do next time, which can be even more valuable than succeeding. Continual practice yields constant improvement in any skillset.

Interpersonal skills are less widely recognized than other kinds of skills, but they're still very important. If you're someone who is very anxious, getting more experience talking to strangers or putting yourself in other situations you've been avoiding can improve your communication skills and help your anxieties fade away. Frequent conversations with friends and strangers alike will make you more charismatic and better at getting your point across. Practicing patience can help you live a calmer, more well-adjusted lifestyle. These are all practical and rewarding skills that can help you achieve several different goals. It can be a bit harder to notice developmental dividends with these kinds of skills, but if you pay attention, you are sure to see the positive results of your efforts. Managing your anxiety can turn a painful experience into a pleasant one, thus lowering your overall stress levels. When you improve your charisma, you will likely notice that people will be more responsive to your ideas. Greater patience allows you to approach issues level-headed, and developmental dividends come in the form of less stress and frustration at relatively minor incidents. These may not be financial dividends, but they are still valuable.

DEVELOPING YOUR RELATIONSHIPS

As you improve your social skills, you will probably find that your relationships will improve as well. It will become easier to hold conversations, even with complete strangers. You will have less trouble finding common ground with those you disagree with, and it will be easier to defuse arguments, turning them into more constructive conversations. You may find yourself forging new relationships or deepening those you already have. These are all great developmental dividends that can drastically improve your experience when it comes to personal relationships.

Remember that relationships take time and investment to build, just like investing in yourself. Don't expect to see results right away, but take notice of the developmental dividends as they appear. Investing in the bonds you form with others is always rewarding, and often you will find friends and family who support and encourage your self-improvement journey.

CHANGING YOUR ATTITUDE

A bad attitude is one of the biggest roadblocks to making progress on your goals. If you lack the determination, dedication, and willpower to work toward a goal, you will likely run out of motivation long before you would otherwise achieve the goal. Luckily, you can improve your attitude and see developmental dividends on your self-investment journey. As your attitude shifts to become more positive and forward-thinking, you will find it easier to put in the work required for self-investment. This work will seem less like a chore and more like a gift you're giving to your future self. Reframing the way you think about success and setting goals can make a huge difference in how likely you are to see your goals through to the end.

Consider whether you have a fixed mindset or a growth mindset. A fixed mindset is rooted in the belief that you have certain things you are good or bad at, and you should focus your efforts on the things you are already good at. It suggests that if you're bad at something, you are wasting your time by trying to improve in that area. In this way, a fixed mindset can be very limiting, as it encourages you to give up on things that at first feel too difficult. Having a growth mindset, on the other hand, means you believe that with enough effort, you can become skilled in any area. You don't need to be naturally gifted to excel in an area; you just need to work at it, and over time your skills will improve. The process of learning and growing is more important than how good or bad you are at something at a given point in time because you know you can become better. A growth mindset is much more empowering than a fixed mindset, and it opens up many more opportunities for you. It is important to cultivate a growth mindset, matched with self-determination, as you continue to pursue your goals.

Adopting a growth mindset gives you developmental dividends in the form of motivation and control. When you start to believe you can improve your skills in any area, not just those you're naturally talented in, you become more motivated to continue investing in yourself. You know the investment will pay off, and you will feel more in control of your life. When you envision your future with a growth mindset, you realize that the ability to shape your life, as you see fit, is in your hands. You are in control of your abilities; therefore, you start to feel more in control of your life's direction. Ultimately, you then begin to live life on your own terms.

HOW DIVIDENDS HELP YOU TAKE CONTROL IN YOUR LIFE

It's hard to stick with something if you don't think it's doing you much good. People give up on diets if they don't see progress in the first couple of days. Those artists who are not naturally talented and lack a growth mindset might give up if their first few sketches look shaky, never knowing what their art could look like if they just stuck with it. Many first-time investors don't wait for their stocks to increase in value, so they sell them too early, losing any value they could have gained from waiting a little longer.

Developmental dividends let you know your efforts are working. Without them, you might be tempted to give up on your goals before you've given yourself enough time to reap the rewards of your efforts. When you start recognizing developmental dividends, you will have the patience to wait for the long-term payoff of all your self-investment labors.

So many people spend their lives looking for their next get-rich-quick scheme. They want to expend as little effort as possible to see the most significant rewards. This is known as the economy of effort principle. It means that people look for the easiest way to complete a task without wasting too much energy, to gain substantial benefits. Precisely, this principle explicitly establishes that it is a good thing to use minimal effort relative to the benefits to be gained. While it might sound nice to do very little and still get rewarded for it, the truth is that you will have better luck putting in the effort for long-term growth than you will if you're only sitting around and waiting for success to come to you. Once you put in the initial effort and have patience, only then will you see your economy of effort improve.

Consider the story of Jamaican Olympian Usain St. Leo Bolt, who is often regarded as the greatest sprinter of all time. He won eight gold medals in three Olympics. He ran for a mere 115 seconds in all of his races combined, and he earned 119 million dollars. However, Usain

Bolt didn't suddenly wake up one day and magically find out he'd become the greatest sprinter overnight. For those less than two minutes he ran in the Olympics, he trained for twenty years. Usain Bolt's story is a classic example of the economy of effort principle. This exact story is shared widely across several social media platforms as motivation for people to patiently invest in what they love, with hopes of obtaining great success and reward in the long run. The time Usain Bolt spent training was his self-investment, and his first couple of wins in non-Olympic events were his developmental dividends. Those wins encouraged him to keep going, training until he was setting records and getting recognized for his skills on a global scale. This is to say, long-term patience pays off. Even if the developmental dividends start small, they will increase exponentially the longer you stick with your self-investment endeavors.

If you want to find success on the same level as Usain Bolt, or if you want to achieve a more modest dream, you cannot wait around for luck. You need to take responsibility for your growth. You must invest in yourself, acknowledge developmental dividends as you receive them, and pay attention to how your efforts are already starting to pay off. Only then will you feel like you are truly in control of your life and your destiny.

7

SELF-EFFICACY

"OVERDRAFTING" ON YOUR POTENTIAL TO BUILD SELF-WORTH

Overdrafting on your potential means you're able to accomplish more than you previously thought possible.

Most people hear the term overdraft and immediately groan. If you overdraft on your bank account, you've taken out more money than you had in the account. This can often come with a fee, which is why most people try to avoid overdrafts. While the general perception is usually negative, overdraft policies serve an essential purpose for both banks and account owners. After all, an overdraft "allows the account holder to continue withdrawing money even when the account has no funds in it or has insufficient funds to cover the amount of the withdrawal" (Kagan, 2020d, para. 1). It is a safety net, not necessarily something to be feared. Without it, you wouldn't be able to complete purchases that require more than the available balance in your bank account. Essentially, the overdraft amount then becomes a loan you have to repay—just like any other loan.

Think of your bank account as an estimate of your potential. In the context of this metaphor, the amount of money in your bank account is equivalent to what you perceive your potential to be. If you don't have a lot of self-worth, your bank account funds may start out very small. You don't feel like you're capable of very much, so perhaps you don't try to put much work toward your goals. Inevitably, you are held back by your fear of an overdraft. But as we discussed, an overdraft isn't always a bad thing. It can help you exceed your initial expectations for yourself. Overdrafting on your potential means you're able to accomplish more than you previously thought possible. Taking risks and pushing yourself past your previous expectations is one of the best ways to improve your self-worth and start recognizing your full potential.

> *"The only person qualified to determine your worth is you!"*
>
> *— @FAIRYSFORUM ON INSTAGRAM*

Success occurs when you convince yourself that you have the abilities and persistence needed to succeed, given enough time and effort. Even if you are not exactly where you need to be, the only thing stopping you from improving your abilities is whether or not you are dedicated to self-investment. This is why self-efficacy—confidence in your ability to regulate your motivation and execute at your utmost potential—is so important. A heightened sense of efficacy increases accomplishment and overall well-being in numerous ways. People with greater assurance in their capabilities perceive complicated responsibilities as challenges to conquer rather than intimidating threats to avoid. Having this same efficacious attitude will allow you to tackle more critical goals while maintaining a strong commitment to ensuring you achieve them. It will also intensify and support your efforts even when failure is feared. And if you fail or had a setback, you will rebound quickly with the ball in your court—now, it is up to you to make the next move.

When you have very little faith in your abilities, it's hard to see just how much potential you really have. It's easy to mistakenly feel like luck is more powerful than you will ever be. Instead of trying a difficult task and risking an overdraft, you might shy away from it altogether because you envision yourself possibly failing. However, if you never try, you will never give yourself the chance to succeed. You need to try challenging tasks to show yourself that you can overdraft on your potential. After all, you are more capable of growth and improvement than you might think.

There are several gaping holes in my recollection. Still, I will never forget when I was selected to join a team of performers who represented Jamaica at the 2012 World Championship of the Performing Arts (WCOPA)—the only global performing arts talent competition held annually in Hollywood, California. Respected American entertainment industry professionals attended the event as judges, seminar presenters, and scouts to sign new talents. I not only saw this experience as a once-in-a-lifetime opportunity to showcase my acting talent on the international stage; it was also an avenue for me to overdraft on my potential. As exciting as this may sound, it was one of the most terrifying moments in my lifetime.

Though I was a recipient of several gold and silver medals for performances at the Jamaica Cultural Development Commission speech and drama festivals, I knew I needed to push myself past my limits to even stand a chance on the international stage. I spent sleepless nights scouring the Internet in search of tips for competing international actors visiting America. I watched countless acting audition videos done in the United States and carefully observed the competition's format by watching videos of previous WCOPA competitors. I worked indefatigably on sharpening my acting skills for the global championship. I practiced, practiced, and practiced even more.

Fast forward, months later, I arrived in Hollywood, and the first preliminary round of the competition had begun. What also began was my battle with my internal fears. Just hours before the first elimination round, there I was, sitting on the cold floor in my hotel room. Terrified. Silence surrounded me. I could hear my stomach's gusty symphony of murmurs and rumbles, and my blood pumping to my head. I started to question my purpose for entering the competition. I told myself I wasn't ready to compete against the top performers from around the world. I feared my English pronunciations would not match up to the standard; I barely knew how to construct proper sentences in English without interjecting some Jamaican patois in the mix.

At age eighteen, I had big dreams. Becoming an actor was one of them. I was also aware of the sustainable value of self-efficacy at that point in my life. A few minutes into my internal thoughts, I got up from the cold floor. Looking in the hotel room mirror, I steeled myself as I spoke powerful words of encouragement. I reminded myself about all the sacrifices made to travel to America for the competition. This understanding propelled me to power through the competition with confidence in my acting talent. I conquered the preliminary rounds with ease and advanced to the semi-finals. I had not qualified to compete in the finale. However, I was awarded a tuition-based scholarship to attend the New York Conservatory for Dramatic Arts.

This experience is one of many where overdrafting on my potential was essential. The ability to measure and regulate my self-worth was crucial for developing my acting skillset for a competition that was alien to me in numerous ways. In a way, I decoded my acting talent in the Jamaican context and juxtaposed it to acting in America, a place and space where such talent is deemed a spectacle. I did this intending to develop and encode a more robust mindset and skillset that was worth pursuing on the international stage. I challenged myself to do well. Mind you, the judges, who were some of the best of the best in the entertainment industry, awarded me a scholarship to further develop my talent. This award cemented the fact that I was capable of much more. In the end, I started to recognize my full potential, even in other areas of my life, and no longer dreaded an overdraft.

Pushing yourself past your initial estimates of your potential will help you develop a sense of self-efficacy. Don't be afraid to overdraft; you will often be pleasantly surprised at your capabilities if you give yourself a chance. Developing a "resilient sense of efficacy requires experience in overcoming obstacles through perseverant effort" (Bandura, 1994, pp. 3-4). Essentially, this means you must try even those tasks that you are not entirely confident about doing. The more you surpass your expectations and overdraft on your potential, the more you will start to see yourself as someone capable of success. The self-worth funds in your metaphorical bank account will grow, and you will acquire interest achieved only through continuous self-investment.

WHY SELF-EFFICACY MATTERS

Your belief in being able to determine the course of your life is worth more than you might think. You need to have confidence that any self-investment you make will pay off. Believing in your ability to make a positive difference in your life and the lives of others is key to achieving this confidence. If you think that your efforts are not worth the time you spend on them, then what's the point of making these investments? If you feel that even if you were the most capable person in the world, you couldn't succeed, there would be no point in investing in yourself. By that logic, no amount of self-investment could possibly help you achieve your goals.

These kinds of beliefs are self-defeating. They convince you that the war has already been lost before the first battle has begun. When you start building your sense of self-efficacy, you begin to see yourself as an active participant in your own life rather than someone who is just being dragged along by luck and fate. You develop more confidence in your abilities, and you see that all the work you're putting in to improve yourself will pay off—if it hasn't already. Likewise, you recognize your potential, and in doing so, you simultaneously increase it in pursuit of vastly greater accomplishments.

DEFEATING THE MINDSET OF HELPLESSNESS

Many people feel helpless in their own lives. They look back on their previous misfortune and believe it will continue regardless of what they do. They see no way to drag themselves out of their current situation and improve their lives using their abilities. Because they lack self-confidence and self-efficacy, they unknowingly create their self-fulfilling prophecy. They don't strive for anything greater than what they already have, and life does not hand them success on a silver platter. They let opportunities pass them by, either because they don't recognize opportunities when they appear or have already decided that no opportunity will benefit them. They are so caught up in every cloud that they never think to look for the silver lining. If you live your life convinced that nothing will get better no matter what you do, then that's exactly what's going to happen.

The truth is that nothing in your life will change until you decide to change it. You are not helpless, so you must choose to act. If you remain passive in your own life, you will miss out on every chance to improve it. When you start believing in your self-efficacy, it becomes natural to look for and make the most out of all the opportunities offered to you. As you keep your goals in mind and commit to becoming more proactive, you will watch your self-investment pay off right in front of your eyes. You will no longer see yourself as helpless and ineffective. Instead, you will recognize the power you wield to change your life, and you will put that power to use.

"Everything in life starts with your mindset first and your actions second. Your actions follow your thoughts, your beliefs, and ideas. To make a shift, to free your energy: start with getting your mind right, and then, take action."

— SYLVESTER MCNUTT III

OVERCOMING OBSTACLES

Everyone faces obstacles that can hold them back from achieving greatness. Some obstacles are very minor. Maybe you want to do two different things that will help you make progress on your goals, but both things are happening simultaneously, and you need to choose one. Maybe someone pushes back against one of your ideas, preventing you from trying out the more efficient method for completing a task. These obstacles may be relatively minor, but they can still set you back a few days or weeks if you don't know how to handle them properly.

On the other hand, you may experience some major obstacles that seem, at first glance, to make success completely impossible. Major obstacles can come in many different forms. You might fail a class or get fired from your job, and you begin to think that your future and financial security will certainly be jeopardized. You could have relationship issues that create a significant disruption in your life. You might develop a physical or mental health condition that could make it harder to work toward the goals you have outlined for yourself.

Even otherwise, positive events can become obstacles in certain contexts. For example, you might need to relocate for employment or to further your education, thus forcing you to prioritize your career goals or an intimate relationship. You get the picture. These and many other obstacles could bring your dreams to an unfulfilling end, but only if you allow them to. If you believe in your self-worth enough to get back on the horse every time you fall off, no obstacle is too great for you to overcome.

Self-efficacy reframes the way you perceive obstacles. Instead of seeing them as enormous, impossible challenges that spell the end of your ambitions, they become more manageable tasks that just require critical thinking and perseverance. The key is to not give up at the first sign of defeat. Instead, keep pushing—even if it means you have to rework your strategy entirely. Sometimes life doesn't go as we plan, but encountering obstacles doesn't mean you've failed. It just means that it's time to try again. If you genuinely believe that you can overcome any obstacle, you will inevitably achieve success.

TAKING INITIATIVE

Initiative is your ability to spring into action without a prompt from anyone else. It means you are ready to act before others so you can pounce on every opportunity that comes your way. As the saying goes, "The early bird gets the worm." By becoming the early bird who is the first to try new things, committing yourself to hard work, and stepping up when it's needed most, you will reap greater rewards than those who choose to wait for good things to come their way.

Taking initiative requires you to be willing to do tasks that others shy away from. If you've committed yourself to self-investment, you have already shown great initiative. Many people reject the idea of improving themselves, content to remain exactly the same as they have always been. Because of this, they are not very likely to achieve great success. To succeed with your own merits, you must be willing to improve. It's not always easy work, but it is rewarding, and it will bring you a much greater return on your self-investment than what you originally put in. When you are confident that your efforts are worthwhile, it's easy to make investments in yourself and leap at every opportunity presented to you. Opportunities don't wait around for very long. If you learn to act fast on an opportunity when it's presented to you, you will end up much better off than if you hesitate and convince yourself to let the opportunity pass.

BUILDING SELF-EFFICACY INTEREST

If you're someone who tends to attribute good and bad events in your life to luck or chance, it can be hard to build up a mentality of trusting yourself. You might struggle with it at first, and it might take you a while to start believing in your self-efficacy. As is the case with most investments, you may not see results right away. But if you start taking steps to show yourself just how capable you are, your mindset will slowly change over time. Eventually, you will begin to see that your actions determine your success. This belief will help you power through any challenge that stands between you and your goals.

Let's revisit the metaphor used earlier to explain this concept. If your bank account is a measure of your potential in your eyes, then your sense of self-efficacy is the interest on that account. When you underestimate your potential, it's hard to generate self-efficacy. You haven't yet convinced yourself that you are capable of great things. However, as you continually overdraft on your potential, you start to see that you are worth more than you once believed. As the measure of your potential increases, so too does your self-efficacy. You have a wealth of experiences that show you that you can achieve much more than you once thought possible, so your confidence grows. You start thinking of yourself as someone who is in control of their life. This process allows you to develop a strong sense of self-efficacy necessary to hinder you from seeing yourself as helpless. It also gives you the conviction you need to take the initiative to leap toward achieving your goals.

CONTINUE THE CYCLE

Self-investment is cyclical! The more you invest in yourself, the better your results, and the more confidence and capability you will generate to invest in yourself once more. This is the same practice you would follow when making any financial investment. As you invest and make more money than you started with, you can re-invest that money and make even more next time.

The same cycle applies to self-efficacy. Once you've started to take notice of the consequences of your actions, good or bad, you can begin to make only those decisions that bring you closer to your goals. At this point, all you need to do is continue the cycle. Keep finding new opportunities to test your mettle, and you will keep surprising yourself with the results of your efforts. As you continue to invest in yourself and experience the positive results of self-investment, your self-confidence will increase in value. If you maintain this cycle—always looking for opportunities to learn and grow—you will start to internalize your self-efficacy and really believe in yourself. Keep expanding your knowledge and skills, continuing the cycle over and over again, and you will never feel your sense of self-efficacy fall short again.

8

SELF-AWARENESS
"CAPITALIZING" ON CREATIVITY

Finding the right balance and getting your imagination to work for you, and not the other way around, will allow you to capitalize on your creative talents.

Creativity is generally viewed as a positive asset. It is a conduit between the ideas that float around in your head and reality. A person who is articulated as creative can often think outside the box and come up with new solutions to old problems. Sometimes, this means they discover a faster way to complete a task, or they come up with an entirely different method that can save time and energy. However, this isn't always the case, especially when creativity is let loose without any restrictions or guidelines. If left unchecked, creativity may not be such an asset, after all.

When I was a child, boredom was outlandish to me. Creativity was my friend at play. As I grew older, I journeyed with my creative juices flowing. I was known among my peers and educators as "the young man with the creative touch" in primary and secondary school, and even university. My experiences have taught me that a little creativity is excellent for solving problems, but too much can lead one astray. In my first year of university, not only did I execute a well-written and thought-provoking book review on Ken Gordon's *Getting It Write: Winning Caribbean Press Freedom*, I also designed, and made by hand, a cover with a bit of finesse for it. A few hours after I had submitted it for grading, my lecturer emailed me saying:

"Michael!!!!! Listen, I saw your book review cover!!!!!! What a cover!! Man, alive! We need to talk. I am serious. We need to talk about your talent. Don't joke with it."

— CH

I had never seen that many exclamation marks in a single body of text prior to this email, nor thereafter. My lecturer was obviously excited that I used my creativity to add flair to the assignment. After assessing the book review, she gave my paper an A-. On the flip side of the coin, I've had lecturers who thought my creativity slightly overpowered my ability to present good enough academic papers. From these experiences, I've learned to gauge my creativity and apply it when suitable.

You need to know thyself! How self-aware are you? Do you know your creative self well enough? I ask these questions to bring to the fore the importance of self-awareness. As you become older, it is your duty to engage with yourself to figure out who you are and identify the multifaceted identities associated with your being. Your creative identity is just as important as any other. As you develop an awareness of your creative self, you will become more self-conscious and objective in your efforts to maximize and measure your skills.

Your creativity may not be necessary for every situation and should not be used to fill the gap of incomplete work. If you have begun to look for only creative ways to complete tasks and save yourself some work, you are doing yourself a disservice. You will miss out on the intrinsic benefits of hard work, and you will lose out on valuable opportunities to cultivate qualities like determination and dedication. Additionally, you might end up putting far more work into coming up with a creative solution instead of just following the one those who came before you created. You can end up completely off-course, spending more of your valuable energy solving a problem you created instead of the one you were initially trying to solve. You might even have many absurd, half-formed ideas that don't actually help you as much as you think. An abundance of creativity often amounts to a series of experiments, which might create additional work and delays in the self-improvement process.

Creativity can have positive or negative effects. It can be an asset or a liability. If you allow it to become more of a liability, you risk your creativity negatively impacting your capital. A bank or financial account's capital is a measure of its assets compared to its liabilities.

Assets are all the things that provide value, and liabilities are all of the expenses the account owes. Positive capital means that the value of your assets exceeds the value of your liabilities.

You want your creativity to be an asset for you, not a liability. You want it to help you think critically about any problems that arise during the self-improvement process. You don't want it to distract you and waste your time by making everything needlessly complicated. Finding the right balance and getting your imagination to work for you, and not the other way around, will allow you to capitalize on your creative talents.

To have your creative gene work in your favor and not against it, you must first understand some of the dangers creativity can pose. This will allow you to look out for common pitfalls, thus helping you save your time and energy so they can be used where they are most needed. Once you understand some of the downsides of letting your creativity run away with you, you can begin to shape it to fit your needs instead.

HOW CREATIVITY CAN GET IN YOUR WAY

When you're improving yourself, you should be aware of every tool in your repertoire and how each of them can help you achieve your goals. Creativity can help, but it is often misused and overused to the point that it becomes a burden rather than a benefit. Too much creativity can trip you up and pull your focus away from your goals. It can become a distraction that keeps you from succeeding, making it harder for you to make significant progress.

Think of creativity like sugar in your morning cup of coffee. If you prefer your coffee sweet and a little different than its natural flavor, a small scoop of sugar goes a long way. Just a little bit can balance out the coffee's natural bitterness. However, if you dump in far too much sugar, you're going to end up with an undrinkable mess. Even people with the biggest sweet tooth wouldn't want to drink a coffee that is almost more sugar than it is liquid. Creativity, like sugar, is best when used in moderation. It is great occasionally and when used in small amounts. If it is used excessively, it doesn't ease the path to success; instead, it obfuscates it, wasting your time and making everything more complicated. Essentially, creativity can jeopardize your success when it is used too liberally because it can pull you off-course and cause you to lose track of your priorities.

CREATING A DISTRACTION

The ability to focus on a task is an incredibly important skill, no matter what you're trying to accomplish. Without focus, we tend to procrastinate, always looking for something else to maintain our attention. Focus allows us to put all of our energy into one task instead of spreading ourselves thin, thereby lowering the quality of our work. I know it's not always easy to keep our focus on a single task. Countless things in our lives provide sources of distraction. We may think about all the other tasks we need to get done and end up working on something less important, or we might get distracted with more fun activities like playing video games or watching TV. It's fine to take breaks when they're needed, but you won't get any work done if your attention keeps slipping away from the task at hand. The last thing we need is to add to the number of things distracting us at any given time, but when we start looking for creative solutions where they're not required, we do precisely that.

Creativity often drives us to experiment instead of sticking to methods that have already been proven effective. When we experiment, we start to focus more on the results of our experiments than we do on how much progress we're making toward our goals. Perfecting these experiments becomes our new goal, and we start focusing on how we can make very minor improvements. The focus we once had for our actual goals all but vanishes.

It is okay to innovate sometimes, but innovation should only ever be in service of our larger goals, not despite them. If it distracts us from the improvements we're trying to make, then it's not actually doing us any favors. Instead of splitting our focus between the standard methods for self-improvement and more creative options, we are often better served by just putting in the work to get things done the old-fashioned way. This keeps our focus where it is most essential and reduces the risk of getting sidetracked, which would only extend the amount of time it will take us to achieve our goals.

MAKING SELF-INVESTMENT OVERLY COMPLICATED

Self-investment isn't exactly a simple process—as everyone's priorities and desired outcomes are different—but it shouldn't be an excessively complex one either. In fact, the basic idea behind self-investment is straightforward. You get what you give, and if you invest in yourself now, you will benefit from it in the future. This simplicity is what makes the process of improving one's self accessible to everyone. Every person can improve, and by cultivating positive traits and developing their skillsets, every person has the capacity for growth. While each person's specific actions to expand their skills and benefit themselves may differ, the general structure is simple and very easy to follow. Why make the process more complicated than it needs to be?

There is no get-rich-quick method when it comes to self-investment. Like any good investment, these things take time, and the most creative solution in the world still isn't likely to save you much time. The honest truth is that you need to be willing to work hard at your goals and be patient enough to wait for them to pay off. Rushing the process and making things overly complicated isn't going to get you better results. You will likely end up accomplishing a small portion of the skills you should learn, or you will distract yourself, adding time to the self-investment process instead of speeding it up.

WASTING YOUR TIME AND ENERGY

Self-investment takes time, but it doesn't need to take forever. Eventually, you should be able to enjoy the results of your hard work. If you get distracted looking for creative ways to improve yourself, how much improvement do you think you will actually make if you waste too much time on side projects and experimental trials? Is this really the best way for you to be using your energy, or could you direct it somewhere it will be more effective?

If you want to maximize your efficiency, you need to consider where your energy will do the most good. Let's say you need to bake and decorate a cake in an allotted time for a celebration. Would it make more sense to spend all of your time making intricate decorations, or should you focus on the cake first and let the decorating come second?

What would happen if you messed up one of these two steps? Which would be the better one to sacrifice? If you don't quite nail the decorations, the negative repercussions are almost nonexistent. Sure, the cake may not look pretty, but you've still got a cake to serve to everyone. If your cake comes out undercooked or burned, or worse, if you end up with no cake at all, it won't matter how good your decorations are. There still won't be anything to eat. Trust me! Duff Goldman, Nancy Fuller, and Lorraine Pascale—judges on the Holiday Baking Championship—would agree. Therefore, it's better to put the most energy into making sure your cake, the foundation of your dessert, comes out great. The decorations are less important, so they are only to be added if you have extra time and energy at the end.

If the self-investment process is like baking a cake, you want to treat it the same way. You want to spend your energy where it will get you the best results, and you want to establish your foundation before you try to decorate it creatively. This is why self-awareness is important. You don't want to put all of your efforts into vastly less important ventures that offer very little return on your self-investment. Focus on making the biggest difference you can with the energy you have, and only worry about adding a creative touch once you've got everything else under control.

HOW TO PROPERLY HARNESS CREATIVITY

Just because you shouldn't entirely rely on creativity doesn't mean it has no place in the self-investment process. You can still use creativity to your advantage as long as you are smart about using it. This primarily means that you should use your creativity in addition to the standard methods for self-investment, not as a replacement. This ensures that you're getting the most out of your efforts to improve, learning the value of hard work and determination, while still giving your self-improvement journey a personal touch. If you use creativity sparingly, it will stay an asset; overuse it, and you risk turning it into a liability.

BRAINSTORM ABOUT YOUR GOALS

One of the best places to apply your creativity is during the process of setting your goals. You may find it helpful during this stage to visualize the dream life you're trying to create for yourself. Think creatively about the kind of future you would like to experience, and consider what kinds of skills and traits you would need to practice in order to achieve that life. Here, you can let your creativity run wild, only reined in by the limits of what you can reasonably expect to achieve—feasibility is key.

There is no harm in being creative here, as you are not at risk of wasting any time. In fact, it's actually beneficial to spend a little time daydreaming for the sake of your motivation. A healthy dose of creativity can help you be aware of the areas you want to improve in, those you might not have thought about otherwise. It can also help you feel more excited about the ways your life will change when you start making and benefiting from these investments. You want to give yourself something to look forward to. Being thoughtfully creative about your future can give you the encouragement you need to genuinely believe you can and will make these changes in your life.

LOOK FOR INEFFICIENT TASKS

When you try to improve specific tasks with creative solutions, make sure you are only attempting to do this for tasks that prove to be inefficient otherwise. Only worry about the tasks that are huge time drains, and don't spend too much effort trying to improve things that generally don't cost you much time or effort regardless. As the old saying goes, "If it's not broken, don't fix it." You will only end up wasting your time, and it's time that could be better spent elsewhere.

Keep in mind how much time you will spend trying to develop a creative solution compared to how much time you would spend doing the task in general. If you find that you might exceed the regular amount of time you'd spend on the task, it's typically better to move on and do things the conventional way. If you're really trying to save time, then there is no reason to persist with an experiment that extends the whole process.

At the end of the day, you want to be aware of maximizing your efficiency. Most of the time, you can do this by maintaining your focus and resisting the urge to get caught up with side projects that don't really benefit you. On very rare occasions, this can mean thinking outside the box about an issue that has you stumped and coming up with a new way to continue progressing toward your goals. If you choose the most efficient option for achieving your goals and keep your creative urge in check, you will benefit the most.

9

SELF-CONSTRUCTION
AVOIDING MORAL "BANKRUPTCY" AND ACTS OF "FRAUD"

Work toward developing a mindset that labels fraudulent practices and moral bankruptcy as wrong, and you will have a much more fulfilling self-improvement journey.

Success isn't only about how much money you make or what kind of job you have. It's also about the way you interact with others and the things you do to succeed. As you work toward your goals, you want to make progress in ways that let you feel good about yourself and your efforts. You must have the right attitude and values when you're pursuing success. If you don't act in line with good morals, you take as many steps backward as you do forward. Hence the need for a moral construction of self.

An important aspect of building one's moral identity is the ability to construct it. You want to carve a path of self-improvement that you can be proud of. If you can't look back on your actions and feel good about them, and if you can't say you've become a better person ethically in the process, then can you really say you've committed to self-improvement? Investing in your future success isn't worth it if your moral character suffers as a result. You ought to construct yourself as an ethical being.

Self-construction is a life design process that enables one to be an agent of self-development and the development of others. You need to utilize this process to create a rigid moral agency that will prepare you to endure disproportionately difficult situations. Your moral agency should be rooted in who you are, and it should also guide your actions. From my experiences, I have learned that self-construction—like self-awareness and other concepts—is a lifelong process. There are times when you may act slightly outside of your moral borderline. In an instance like this, the onus is on you to reconstruct your moral self to prevent faltering on your self-investment journey.

There is a common misconception that in order to succeed where others have faltered, you need to act ruthlessly. People who believe this see compassion and kindness as weaknesses. They see no value in helping their fellow man. It is a solitary, pessimistic way to look at life. Are these people really correct? It may be true that you can rise to success a bit faster by stepping on the backs of others, but is this the kind of life you want to lead? Will you feel good about what you've done, or will you feel guilty, remorseful, and lonely? Poor morals and immoral practices might bring you financial or material success faster, but they're not worth executing. They sabotage your emotional well-being and your relationships. Once you reach the top, you're going to look around you and realize you don't have anyone to share your success with. What's the point of all the hard work you put in if you end up alone at the end of it? If you have burned all your bridges and taken advantage of others until you've lost everyone's support, all the material wealth in the world won't be able to make you happy.

As you work your way toward success, you want to avoid things that could be articulated as moral bankruptcy and fraud. Bankruptcy means you are entirely lacking in some areas. It's typically used to refer to a company losing all of its money, but it can also mean a deficiency in fundamental traits, like integrity and determination. Morally bankrupt people are likely to lie, cheat, and steal their way to success, to the detriment of others. They are more likely to commit fraud. Fraudulence is the act of deceiving someone by lying to them or cheating them. It involves knowingly committing hoaxes to harm others in order to help yourself. Your self-investment efforts will greatly benefit if you don't consider unethical acts to get ahead in life.

In the stock market, deceptive practices such as stock fraud and investment fraud are common. In instances where these fraudulent schemes are successful, investors are usually induced to purchase stocks based on false information. These organized schemes are categorized as white-collar crimes and are punishable by law. Though you might not experience legal repercussions for committing fraud, in most cases, the negative consequences of sabotaging your relationships and making a bad name for yourself should be enough to deter you. Work toward developing a mindset that labels fraudulent practices and moral bankruptcy as wrong, and you will have a much more fulfilling self-improvement journey. Real self-investment means becoming a better person, and you can't do that while practicing moral bankruptcy and acts of fraud.

Your moral compass ought to be pointed in the right direction!

I experienced a dose of moral bankruptcy in a very subtle way in university, when I plagiarized my first assignment, thinking it was OK. Yes, I plagiarized. Copy! Paste! Print! It was that simple.

The tendency I had to engage in the criminal act of literary theft began in high school. I didn't know better. At that time, training about plagiarism was never in my high school's teaching curriculum. To complete written assignments, projects, and group presentations, I would copy, paste, and present information from various Internet sources—as my own. As I transitioned into the twelfth and thirteenth grade—what we call sixth form in Jamaica—I was introduced to copying and pasting the links of websites onto a citation page, and I thought that would suffice as referencing. Little did I know I was involved in what is classified as an act of fraud. I was never penalized; neither was I warned about my actions. If you asked any of my classmates during that period what it means to copy and paste information from the Internet without giving credit to the author, their answer would more than likely be "research." I was conducting research. That is exactly what I interpreted the process to be.

I felt confident transitioning into university, knowing that completing assignments would be as simple as finding, copying, pasting, editing, and submitting online for grading. I was wrong! The University of the West Indies, Mona, like many other universities, has a strict policy that forbids plagiarism; any UWI student found guilty of presenting another person's material as their own would be punished. I was puzzled. How could something that seemed so right in secondary school be frowned upon at the tertiary level?

The very first writing assignment I received at UWI, Mona, required me to write a reflective essay about my experience as a student of English in high school—and I plagiarized. Though my professor, Dr. Jones, wanted me to share snippets from my own experiences, the temptation to plagiarize hindered me from using my own ideas. I vividly recall sitting cross-legged on the bed in my dorm room with my back against the cold wall, and my eyes pierced into my laptop. It was getting late, and I was exhausted. As I yawned and stretched, I noticed the minute hand on my wristwatch was a few minutes shy of eight o'clock. That evening, I typed quite a few keywords into Google and clicked *search* multiple times. I skimmed through several essays on other students' past experiences with English in high school, and I copied bits and pieces from a few of them—of what I thought would form a great composition, with some of my own words in the mix. Period. I completed "my" essay in less than three hours. After careful revision, I felt confident enough that I had compiled a well-organized essay, so I uploaded it to Turnitin—a plagiarism detection software—for grading.

In the next seminar class, Dr. Jones called me aside and said, "Your essay was very colorful!" I smiled, thinking it was meant to be a commendable remark. She then presented me with a hard copy of my essay, and the colorfulness she was referring to became apparent. My smile quickly turned into a frown. "The highlights you see in different colors are proof that you have stolen the majority of what you have presented in this essay from the Internet," she expressed. I hung my head in shame. I did not know whether an apology would be accepted, so I kept silent. There was an extended moment of silence before I heard her mutter under her breath, "This does not look good for a first attempt." Luckily, I was not expelled, nor did I face any serious disciplinary actions. However, I was warned about the possible outcomes if it was to happen again. In that class, I was taught how to do proper citation and referencing. Furthermore, I received remedial academic writing assistance from Dr. Jones on many occasions, even after completing the foundation writing course, which helped sharpen my research and critical thinking skills.

When I was identified as a plagiarizer, that label stripped every ounce of writing confidence I had in me. It belittled my moral self and made it seem as though I lacked ethics. Though the experience made me feel this way, I focused on success ahead and took all the help I could get to tackle academic writing by its horns and rekindle my writing confidence.

From that experience, I learned what plagiarism is and why it should not be condoned—under no circumstances. My understanding of how to conduct research and prepare papers for academic purposes was enhanced significantly. For sure, this experience has helped make my self-improvement journey in academics and other areas much more fulfilling. Since then, I have consistently improved my moral portfolio to avoid weakening my integrity.

NEGATIVE TRAITS TO AVOID

When you think of a good person, what kind of traits do they display? Perhaps more importantly, what kind of characteristics do they *not* display? You remember nice things that others have done for you, but the things they do that negatively impact you tend to stand out far more in your memory. When other people judge your character, your good and bad qualities are juxtaposed. Too many bad qualities can hinder the good qualities you possess from shining, so you want to discourage yourself from adopting these negative traits.

Of course, some character flaws are worse than others. Some may be minor annoyances but ultimately forgivable offenses, while others can interfere with your ability to succeed and impact how others perceive you. They can all be bad in particular circumstances, but certain traits have a more significant impact on your character and morals. The characteristics that are most aligned with moral bankruptcy and acts of fraudulence include being deceitful, self-centered, lazy, and arrogant. These traits will directly interfere with your attempts to become a better, more successful person.

DECEITFULNESS

Deceitful people have no reservations about tricking others. They are willing to do whatever they need to guarantee their own success, even at the expense of the well-being of others. They will lie and cheat their way to the top, and they will rarely make apologies for their behavior. All the while, they will justify their actions by internalizing that they needed to get ahead of the competition. They think they have to drag others down to uplift themselves.

Listen, duplicitous traits hinder success! Drop them!

Despite what some people preach, you don't need to trick others so that you can guarantee personal victory. If you put in hard work of your own, you won't have to rely on deceit and cheating to get your way. You can succeed on your own merits, and success earned this way is always more rewarding than success achieved through deception. Imagine you're running in a competitive race. You have two options: You could try to win the race by training hard every day, slowly building up your stamina and your physical fitness, or you could try to win by tricking and sabotaging your competitors. Both options have a chance of succeeding, but they don't both yield the same outcome. If you use deceit, you have no reason to be proud of your victory. You didn't earn it; you just made it impossible for others to succeed. If you choose to train, you invest in yourself and increase your potential. Even if you don't win the race, you have already improved, both physically and morally. This is more valuable than any competition won through deceit.

Honesty and integrity are more rewarding!

It's also important to recognize that deceit comes in many different forms. Sometimes, deception may be something calculated very blatantly in an attempt to harm others. Other times, it may be a subtle manipulation or white lie you hardly notice you've told. Work to recognize these smaller moments of deceit too, and correct them when they occur before it's too late.

SELF-CENTEREDNESS

To be self-centered is to not care about the well-being of anyone else. There is a big difference between putting your needs first and being self-centered. It's not a bad thing to look out for yourself. In fact, self-investment helps you do precisely this. You can't help anyone else until you've helped yourself. So, there's nothing wrong with taking time to focus on your goals and what makes you feel fulfilled. The problem arises when you also disregard the feelings of others, uncaring of the impact you may have on their lives. If you are not bothered when you hurt someone else's feelings, make unreasonable demands on their time, or fail to support them, you may be engaging in this toxic trait.

Being self-centered can interfere with your ability to build and maintain healthy relationships. People notice when they're being mistreated or when they feel like they have been slighted. If you are too preoccupied with yourself, you may not be as discerning, and you may suddenly find yourself growing apart from people you once considered good friends. If you can't put energy into a relationship in order to maintain it, neither will the other person. If you allow your relationships to erode over time, sooner or later, you will have no one to turn to, or better yet, to consult. You won't have anyone to support you when you need it most, which can cause you to falter on your way to success. To forge relationships that last, you must be willing to consider other people's feelings and be as supportive of them as you would want them to be of you.

LAZINESS

Laziness is the killer of forward momentum! When you allow laziness to hold you back, you give up on your agency and reduce your chances of achieving your goals. You stop making progress, effectively coming to a standstill, and letting the world pass you by. Laziness keeps you from making the most of the opportunities the world presents to you. It causes you to look at challenges and decide they are too hard, even to attempt. When you do this, you never get to find out your true potential.

Laziness should not be confused with exhaustion. It's not lazy to need a break every now and then. Taking breaks is healthy for you. They keep you energized and help you avoid burnout. After your break, you can get right back to work. However, if these breaks continue to drag on far past what's reasonable, and if you find yourself procrastinating your work, you probably have laziness to blame. At this moment, you are well-rested, but you lack the motivation to keep working, possibly because you fail to see the positive outcome that awaits you.

"Procrastination is a lazy man's apology."

— *CHINUA ACHEBE*

You may also have a problem with laziness if you tend to push off your work onto others' shoulders. As a result, it becomes unfair to claim that you are making progress toward your goals when it's not you doing the work. Even if you achieve what you set out to accomplish by doing this, you didn't contribute to it; you took advantage of what others did. This may not really be a true reflection of you, but if you've ever participated in a group presentation, you know exactly who I am talking about. Instead of investing in themselves, they commit self-sabotage, depriving themselves of the lessons they would have learned had they opted to work as a group instead of being lazy.

Defeating laziness involves shifting your mindset so you can see the inherent value of effort. A victory achieved without any hard work is hardly a victory at all. It is much more fulfilling to work toward a goal yourself than to let others do it for you or give up on the goal entirely. Once you start investing effort in what you do, you will see how you're investing in your own development at the same time.

ARROGANCE

In order to see self-investment as a worthwhile pursuit and make the most of it, you need to recognize that you have room to improve. You don't have to be consistently critical of yourself, but you do have to accept that there are certain things you could be performing better at and still others you have yet to learn. However, arrogance can blind you to this realization. It can make you reject the idea of investing in yourself because you believe you already have all the skills you need to achieve your goals. This can leave you utterly unprepared for the actual process of working toward your goals, as you are so used to relying on your limited abilities, and you have little experience working to build your skills.

Arrogance is especially damaging because it causes you to reject the help of others. When you think you are already more than capable than someone else of taking on any challenge, you ignore the role that friends and family play in your life. You start to believe you can handle everything on your own, which may lead you to reject help even when it's in your best interest. Eventually, you are going to come upon a task that you can't manage. You will need someone else's assistance, or even just a supportive friend to encourage you. If your arrogance has progressed to the point that you have driven other people away, you may turn to look for help and find no one there.

REINFORCING THE RIGHT VALUES

If the traits mentioned above, along with others that promote moral bankruptcy, are ones to avoid, then how do you identify and live by acceptable values instead? First, you should focus on identifying positive traits that you'd like to practice yourself. These might include self-reflection, commitment, a positive mindset, honesty, and similar values. Once you've identified these traits, you should also figure out why they are so beneficial to you. Maybe they keep you from making mistakes, or they motivate you to learn new skills. These ethical values might also help you feel like a better person, one who's done a lot of reflection and personal growth. Being a genuine, hard-working person feels good, and other people will enjoy your company. Look at how these positive values affect your relationships and your overall happiness compared to the way negative traits do, and you will see just why they are so important. With this knowledge, you will find it very easy to drop toxic traits and maintain positive ones.

PAY ATTENTION TO THE CONSEQUENCES OF YOUR ACTIONS

Everything we do affects our lives in one way or another. We might see the effect right away, as evident as spilling a glass of water and seeing the immediate impact of getting the floor wet. Or, it might take us a while to see the results of our actions, like mold that builds up under wet floorboards and is only revealed months after it has been left to grow. Regardless of when these consequences occur—they do occur, and recognizing such is the first step toward identifying and replacing negative traits.

Pay attention to what happens when you express one of the negative traits listed previously. How do you feel afterward? How do others feel when they are affected by your actions or learn about them? Are you living in a way that you can be proud of, and that makes others proud? If not, consider why that is. You will probably notice that whenever you act in a way that is deceitful, arrogant, lazy, or self-centered, there is a negative consequence. It may interfere with your self-investment, or it may disrupt a relationship. You will also probably notice that whenever you are kind, determined, and honest, your moral character is repaid in some way, even if it's only through feeling good about yourself. Look at the values you hold that have positive or negative effects on yourself and others, and try to maximize the number of positive outcomes. Before long, you will see the toxic traits that would sabotage your life become less and less frequent, and those admirable traits that make you feel good about yourself will emerge as more and more prominent.

ACCEPT THAT YOU NEED HELP

More often than not, toxic traits stem from an inability to ask for help. You might see yourself as a lone wolf that doesn't need others to succeed, or you might be too nervous about requesting help when you need it most. Either of these two attitudes can interfere with your life's plans. Some self-reliance is good, but not if it's motivated by arrogance or fear.

We all need other people in our lives. Our connection to others is what gives our lives meaning and value. As we grow and develop as people, we should make sure that our relationships are growing and developing as well. This means reaching out to friends and family when we need support and advice, and it also involves repaying the favor when they need help. No one can go through life alone and feel truly fulfilled. If our toxic traits leave us with a poor reputation and very few allies on our quest for a successful life, we probably won't experience contentment even if we succeed.

Investing in yourself also means investing in your long-term happiness. Achieving our goals is a hollow victory if we ruin our relationships along the way. We need to be able to feel proud of what we've done and the road we took to get there. This means cultivating the right values and keeping ourselves on the right path. This is the type of self-construction we need to undergo!

10

SELF-TRUST

RECOUPING FROM FAILED PERSONAL "TRANSACTIONS"

Don't try to fail; try despite the chance you might fail.

Self-trust is an attribute many people lack these days. It is an effervescence of every present confidence that boosts one's decision to refuse to give up on *self*. Though self-trust and self-confidence are closely related, they are not the same thing. Belief in oneself is the driving force that develops the trust we need to rely on our capacity to handle life as it comes at us. If you are to function as an autonomous person, you need to understand and practice self-trust. It will be very hard for you to trust yourself if you continuously pinpoint only your problems. We are all accountable for mentally documenting the reasons why we are flawed, broken, and messed-up.

"I lack confidence, so I can't do it."

"I'm a failure…a delinquent…too much of a neat freak."

These kinds of thoughts pick away at your self-trust. We can't always reveal all that's wrong with ourselves. We need to affirmatively believe that we are good just the way we are and trust in ourselves that we can work to fix whatever we see as wrong.

Failure doesn't mean you've lost and that all your efforts have gone to waste. This can sound a little paradoxical at first. After all, you're probably used to fearing failure. Failing is that terrifying possibility that keeps you up at night and keeps you working hard throughout the day. You want to avoid failure at all costs, don't you? Actually, avoiding failure can do a lot more damage than embracing it ever could. When you avoid failure, you hold yourself back from attempting anything. You don't want to risk the possibility that you might not come out on top, so you choose not to try at all. This might make you feel better in the short-term, but it isn't great for your long-term success. If you can't take a risk or if you never make the initial investment in yourself because you are too afraid of failing, you will never have the chance to prove your doubts wrong.

"It's fine to celebrate success, but it is more important to heed the lessons of failure."

— *BILL GATES*

Failure is, above all else, an opportunity to learn. Like all learning opportunities, we should try to make the most of it when we can. This doesn't necessarily mean that you should pursue failure instead of success. Instead, it means that you shouldn't fear failure when it happens. Don't try to fail; try despite the chance you might fail. Put yourself out there. Try things outside of your comfort zone, and stop letting the fear of failure hold you back. You will often surprise yourself with the results, and even if you do end up stumbling a little, all is not lost. Failure is temporary, and you always have the option to recover from it. The only truly permanent form of failure is when you stop trying.

When you fail, you might be tempted to give up on whatever you were trying to do. That failed transaction can leave you with a bruised ego, making you feel uncertain of your skills and unwilling to risk a second failure. Instead of quitting when you get knocked down, you are better off getting up, dusting yourself off, and using what failure has taught you to your advantage. It can be hard to recognize everything you've learned if you're caught up in the rush of emotions. But once you settle down and take a step back, it is much easier to see exactly where you went wrong. Take note of mistakes you made in your first attempt, as well as moments when you lacked the skills necessary to complete a task to the best of your abilities. Next time you attempt to achieve your goals, use this information to your advantage. Fix any errors and try again. At the very least, you will see an improvement from the last time. Resist the urge to beat yourself up over the mistakes you make along the way. It can take many tries to get a single task right, but if you keep learning and improving on each attempt, you will eventually find the success you've been looking for.

There are many instances in my life where I have failed several times to accomplish a milestone I initially set out to achieve. One experience

I will never forget takes me back to when I developed a burning desire to become a Jamaica 4-H Club Champion Boy of the Year. To attain this title, I needed to have a strong agricultural project, be aware of the history of the 4-H movement, be mindful of current affairs at the time, and display leadership attributes. To vie for the champion 4-H Clubbite of the Year, one must advance to the national level after competing in their parish competition.

I was only thirteen when I first entered the competition; I was a freshman in high school. It was 2007, and this small-in-stature seventh-grade boy had entered a competition against young men who were noticeably older than he was. I did not allow the size of the other competitors to neither intimidate me nor hinder my desire to accomplish such a big title. I entered the interview room with every ounce of confidence I had. I wholeheartedly believed my project to restore 4-H Club activities in my community was very well laid out and explained in my project book. There was no question too hard for me to answer. Besides, I recited the 4-H Club's motto, philosophy, pledge, and creed without stumbling over the words. I exited the interview with my head held high. A few hours later, I found out I was victorious in my parish and was named Clarendon's 4-H Boy of the Year. I was thrilled!

The next leg of the competition was the big league. I needed to up my game to compete against thirteen other young men who were champions for their respective parishes. I updated my project book to include the progress I had made on restoring 4-H Club activities in my community. I ensured I kept up-to-date with local and international affairs. On competition day, I was nervous, to say the least. I was sweating profusely under the salty, hot tent that housed competitors and patrons. Perspiration caused the thin white shirt of the 4-H uniform to stick to my skin. When I entered the interview room, I covered up my anxiety as best as I could with a flash of my teeth every now and then. I did the best I could. I placed second. Not a bad placement, but I had failed to accomplish my ultimate goal.

"To make the best better" is the 4-H Club's motto. Guided by this motto, I contemplated entering the competition the following year. Fear haunted me.

What if you do not win the parish leg of the competition?

What if when you advance to the national round, you are not placed among the top three?

My internalized fear was asking good questions, but my answer was not to throw in the proverbial towel. I responded with a comeback. I got up, dusted myself off, and entered the competition again in 2008 and was awarded as my parish champion once more. However, that year, the 4-H Club decided to change the format of the competition. A regional elimination round was added to allow only three young men from across the island to advance to the finale. I was never one of the three. I placed second in the central region, and my fear began to actualize even more.

I was determined to win the National 4-H Boy of the Year title, so I conquered my fears and entered again in 2009. This time around, I advanced to the regional round and was awarded third place. A step down from my placement the previous year. I was frustrated. The cheerfulness I entered the competition with melted as tears of disappointment rained down my face. I wanted to advance to the national competition so badly.

What have I done wrong?

Did I mix up one of the years?

Did I miss a word or a line in the 4-H creed?

Did I forget to add the title to someone's name?

As those thoughts loomed before me, another idea cast an even larger shadow—*is my intellect being watered down?*

I left the competition venue feeling defeated. I hardly wanted to tell anyone what my placement was. I was embarrassed. That experience caused me to struggle with a bruised ego. At that time, I was unwilling to risk being a failure times four.

I remember having a less than a serious-type conversation with Mr. Annakie—my social studies teacher in high school—about my 4-H Club involvement. He wanted to know why I continued to enter the same competition, even after failing to cop the national title on three attempts. Becoming the all-island 4-H Clubbite of the Year was the goal I set out to achieve, so I explained this to him. "Well, it's not your year," Sir Annakie said jokingly. Though he was poking fun at my defeat, he expressed something I will never forget. He said, "Do not value winning or losing over the process that led to your placements." He was right. I needed to focus on the lessons learned from all my previous attempts to properly prepare for the next time I enter the competition.

I decided not to enter the competition in 2010. I took the time to recalibrate so that I could be a much stronger competitor the following year. I did not give up on myself.

In 2011, when I was seventeen years old, I entered the competition again. I was hungry for the win! Starting that year, they no longer held the regional competition, and I advanced straight to the national achievement day event. There I competed against thirteen other boys —like I did on my first attempt—and was victorious as the Jamaica 4-H Club Champion Boy of the Year. A prestigious title that required me to act as a role model and an ambassador in various capacities for the 4-H Clubs across Jamaica for a year. Perseverance and triumph ensued as a result of my failure.

Pia Wurtzbach, a beauty queen from the Philippines, encountered failure on her quest to become a Miss Universe titleholder. She competed in Binibining Pilipinas three times, and on her third attempt, she won and advanced to the international competition where she was crowned Miss Universe 2015. Pia deprived failure of the opportunity to dictate her standards and control her destiny. Despite contemplating the possibility of losing again in her home country, her persistent nature and self-trust led her on an unwavering risk-taking journey. In the end, she was the victor.

Though everyone's experiences with failure may differ, the internal conversations are certainly similar. If you don't let failure *de*motivate you and water down your trust in you, there is hardly anything you cannot accomplish given enough attempts. If failure has caused you to suffer in the past, trust and believe that it will make you a better individual by increasing your value. If you foster a symbiotic relationship between each of your failed attempts and your reattempts to succeed, you will discover epiphanies as you continue to persist. Never give up on your dreams. Let the famous saying, "If at first you don't succeed, try again" be a light when the dark and dreary clouds of failure hover above you.

HOW FAILURE CAN LEAD TO SUCCESS

Failure feels a lot more final than it actually is. It feels like your journey has come to an end. In reality, failure is just another stepping stone on the way to success. You just need to think about it the right way and allow your experience to teach you. If you picture your success as investing in a stock, failure is less like selling the stock at a loss and more like the moment when the stock hits a lower price. Sure, you can choose to cut your losses and sell your stock, but if you give up, you let go of the chance of future success. If you hold on to your stock, there is a chance that it will go up in value again. If you sell too early, you miss out on this potential future gain.

Failure actually helps to prepare you for success. When you fail, you see why your first attempt went wrong. You know what happens if you try the method you've already used, and if you think critically, you can usually figure out why things went so poorly for you. This information is invaluable. With it, you can completely change your approach. You can increase the likelihood that you will succeed because you now know what methods don't work, and you will avoid them the next time. With enough attempts, you will figure out what went wrong, correct your mistakes, and improve until you can clear any obstacle with ease.

THE POWER OF PATIENCE

Benefitting from failure requires you to be patient. You're going to make mistakes, and it can be tiring and frustrating to keep attempting the same task until you find success. You will likely feel like you're making very little progress with some trials, especially if you start losing patience and rush into things without taking time to reflect on why you failed in the first place. Self-investment is a long-term endeavor, and it requires you to have enough patience to play the long game. Patience is a virtue, and nowhere is that more true than when you're on your fifth attempt at achieving the same goal. *Whew!*

If you're someone who has trouble being patient, it can help to focus on the improvements you make with each successive attempt. Every time you start over, you get a little further than you did last time. You make a bit more progress or learn something new, even if you only learn what not to do. These are valuable assets, and they make these repeated attempts worthwhile. These are not monotonous trials that result in the same thing every time. Turn your gaze to the small improvements in your strategy and the slightly better results you get each time, and you will have the patience for a hundred trials.

TURNING FAILURE INTO FAME

Maybe you're starting to see how failure can be a useful tool, but you still have your doubts. In that case, it can help to look at an example of someone who turned a huge failure into unbelievable success. Not only did they fail before they succeeded, but their failure directly contributed to their future success and made it possible. There are actually hundreds of these kinds of stories if you look at the biographies and histories of famous entrepreneurs and experts in their fields. However, Michael Jordan's story does well at exemplifying the benefits of failure.

When you think of Michael Jordan, failure probably isn't the first thing that comes to mind—and for a good reason. He is one of the most well-known and celebrated basketball players of all time, and he definitely has the winning record to back it up. To say Michael Jordan is good at basketball would be an extreme understatement. Despite that, Jordan wasn't always the legend we all know him to be. Back in high school, Jordan hadn't yet developed the skills that would make him a renowned basketball star. In fact, he didn't even make it on his school's team.

Did this failure end with Jordan vowing never to play basketball again? If it did, we wouldn't be talking about him right now! Jordan attributes his determination to train and improve his skills to a professional level to this initial failure and many more that have followed. Of failure, Jordan once said, "I have missed more than 9,000 shots in my career. I have lost almost 300 games. On twenty-six occasions I have been entrusted to take the game-winning shot, and I missed. I have failed over and over and over again in my life. And that is why I succeed" (Aronson, n.d., para. 7). Every time Jordan thought about how he wasn't skilled enough to make the team, he doubled his efforts to improve his skills until he had what it took. Every time he missed a shot, he became more determined to correct his mistakes and sink the next one. Jordan's efforts clarify just how beneficial failure can be as a motivational tool and a learning opportunity.

If you change your mindset, failure goes from a *de*motivating occurrence to an incredibly powerful motivator. Examine the experiences you've gained from your failed attempts and the frustration you feel from not succeeding, and work to transform them into positive forces. Next time you experience a failed transaction, try to follow in the footsteps of Michael Jordan. You might not become a basketball legend, but you can use the same methods to improve in any field. Use your failure to fuel your future success, and no matter what you do, don't let a temporary failure turn into a permanent defeat.

III
SELF-UPGRADE IN PROGRESS...

11

SELF-CARE

YOUR SELF-INVESTMENT "AGENDA" GUIDE

Your self-investment agenda shows you where to invest your time and energy for the greatest return on your investments. It helps you identify the tasks and attitudes that are most beneficial in your pursuit of success.

Any significant investment strategy starts with a plan. You need to know where you're headed before you can start making changes. Strategic plans help you figure out what's most important to you and what steps you have to take to achieve those goals. This phase of your life is entrenched in the concept of self-care. It is simply taking care of yourself. In relation to self-investment, it means prioritizing and engaging in activities that are good for your personal development, and that will help you progress toward your goals. You are to outline specific self-care goals and make them habits.

If someone struggles with debt and wants to turn their financial situation around, most financial advisers will suggest they make a financial plan. This outline gives them a better idea of what got them into their current debt situation and what they can do about it going forward. A more structured definition of a financial plan highlights that it is "a document containing a person's current money situation and long-term monetary goals, as well as strategies to achieve those goals" (Kagan, 2020b, para. 1). By following a financial plan, people can go from struggling with expenses to generating enough income to start saving the excess.

To make the best use of your time when you're investing in yourself, you need to craft a plan of your own—be guided by your own agenda. Your self-investment agenda shows you where to invest your time and energy for the greatest return on your investments. It helps you identify the tasks and attitudes that are most beneficial in your pursuit of success. The right self-investment plan mixed with an appropriate amount of effort can significantly increase the remuneration you get from your self-investment toils.

In high school, I had my mind pinned on participating in every competition I was qualified to enter. I would always spend a couple of minutes eyeballing my reflection in the mirror at home before traveling to competition venues. I would also talk to myself. I used this ego-fulfilling pre-competition ritual to make promises to myself. I remember promising myself that I would create a plan that would have me exert significant efforts daily to improve myself. Just before the 2010-2011 academic year began, I drafted my own self-investment plan. I knew it would be unrealistic to imagine a better future or perform at a more advanced standard without a feasible system that would allow me to grow successfully. Not only did my plan include goals I wanted to achieve, and the timeline by which I wanted to achieve them, it also had simple, yet valuable, responsibilities that inevitably led me closer to attaining a more holistic life. Because of that plan, my talents improved, accomplishments skyrocketed, my personal fulfillment was amplified, and my confidence in my plan's ability to effect change was actualized.

Essentially, where you will be positioned, and the magnitude to which you will perform tomorrow, will chiefly depend on what you do to improve and care for yourself today.

YOUR CHECKLIST FOR SUCCESS

There are so many different ways you can invest your energy every day. You want to expand and refine your skills, but you also want to learn more about the world around you and work more efficiently. Without a plan, it can be a struggle to keep up with all of these different goals. However, with some proper organization, it becomes easy to make sure you're improving in a well-rounded and consistent manner.

Here is a checklist you can use to direct your time and energy where they are most needed to ensure you get the best results. Think of these suggestions as twenty-three of several other responsibilities you ought to accomplish to ensure you're making progress toward your goals.

1. INVEST IN YOURSELF FIRST AND FOREMOST

This probably isn't something you want to hear, but it's a necessary lesson to learn. If you're young and you're still finding your place in the world, don't put so much focus on serious relationships. Focus on self-improvement first. You have an uncertain future, you probably have little to no financial wealth, and you may not even be entirely sure of who you are and what you want out of life. The last thing you want to do is to try to figure yourself out while also trying to figure someone else out. Until you're somewhere more stable, don't worry about serious commitment. Instead, focus on your education and career. You can still date and try out a few relationships, but your primary focus should be yourself, not a long-term committed relationship that you're not quite ready for.

2. MOTIVATE YOURSELF WITH PODCASTS

If you find yourself lacking motivation, podcasts are a great resource. Podcasts allow you to listen to advice from experts in almost every single industry. You can learn insider information about the kind of skills you should invest in to be a cut above the rest of the competition. You can also listen to podcasts themed around self-help and motivation for an extra boost in confidence and productivity.

The great thing about podcasts is that you can listen to them as you do other things. You can play one through your headphones as you go for a walk or jog. You can leave one running while you do the dishes or fold your laundry. As long as you are doing something simple enough to pay attention, you can fill these otherwise dull moments with valuable information, making them a very low-risk and a high-reward way to invest your time.

3. READ MORE

Reading is another excellent way to learn about new things and expand your knowledge. You're already investing time into knowledge expansion by reading this very book, but don't stop here! The more books you read, the more you know, and the more you improve your chances of success.

If you want to know where to get started, I'd recommend picking up *How Successful People Think* by John Maxwell. In this book, Maxwell reveals the incredible power that our mentality and thoughts have over our lives. We can become more successful just by changing our mental habits, trusting that everything else will follow. This is incredible advice that you might miss out on if you don't start reading more!

"An investment in knowledge always pays the best interest."

— *BENJAMIN FRANKLIN*

---

4. SAVE MORE MONEY

It's very easy to spend impulsively. After all, advertisements are everywhere. If we turn on the TV, we see countless ads for everything from cheap fast food to extravagantly expensive cars. If we spend carelessly on unimportant things we don't need, we won't have any money left when we want to make a purchase that will help us achieve our goals. Get into the habit of saving, and you will always have a financial cushion to fall back on when you need it.

This is easy for me to suggest but not so easy for you to do. I understand. There are times when you have all intentions to save, but something seems to always pop up. In reality, the only way you'll start to save is if you prioritize your needs above your wants. Allow saving to become a priority. Modifying your spending habits is one of the easiest ways for you to be serious about saving. For example, you can follow my lead and cancel subscriptions you rarely use and consider splitting the cost of an upgraded version of a subscription with friends or family members. Another way to save is to avoid purchasing name brand items. Generic brands cost less money, and they work just as good as name brands. You should also make an effort to open a savings account at your local bank. In the end, it's not the amount of money you earn—what is really important is how you budget and save.

Saving money also helps us practice discipline, which is a great skill to cultivate. When we save, we cut down on our tendency to make impulsive decisions as we learn to weigh the long-term value of purchases in our minds before we make them. By exercising this small discipline every day, we achieve the control necessary to stick to our self-investment efforts over time.

5. STOP WASTING TIME

Distractions are everywhere in our lives. There are many time drains we engage in every day that cut down on the amount of time we have available to do more meaningful things. Identify familiar sources of wasted time in your life and make an effort to regulate them. Even deciding only to watch TV after a particular time every night, or to turn off your computer an hour before you go to bed, can help you use your time more efficiently.

A popular way that many people waste time is by using social media. These social networking sites are programmed to manipulate and encourage us to keep scrolling infinitely, as a myriad of new posts pop up every second. If we're not careful, we could lose hours to mindless social media scrolling every week. These are hours that could be utilized more efficiently, so ditch social media—every now and then— and return your focus to more productive endeavors.

6. PAY ATTENTION TO THE NEWS

It's crucial to stay up-to-date with current affairs, both locally and globally. Current events impact your life, whether you recognize their influence or not. Even things that happen halfway across the world can have a ripple effect that reaches you—#**globalization**. A dry spell in one area of the globe could result in a worldwide shortage of a particular crop. A political event in one country could affect business in a country it trades with. Staying informed won't help you prevent these events from occurring, but it will help you anticipate the consequences of each situation and propel you to take appropriate action. If you keep an eye on the news, you can be proactive instead of reactive, and this will save you a lot of time and money in any business. On top of this, it's just a good idea to have a grasp of important global events. Your awareness of current affairs will help you become a more knowledgeable person and ensure that if such topics were to come up in a conversation, you know how to tackle the discourse with your own opinion.

If a constant influx of bad news stories depresses you, just remember:

"In a world filled with hate, we must still dare to hope. In a world filled with anger, we must still dare to comfort. In a world filled with despair, we must still dare to dream. And in a world filled with distrust, we must still dare to believe."

— MICHAEL JACKSON

---

7. ACQUIRE A FORMAL EDUCATION

Formal education helps in just about every field. Depending on the area you want to work in, you may need a degree. If so, formal education is mandatory, but it still has its perks aside from the fancy piece of paper and the line on your resume. Even if you're someone who hates school, be mindful that pursuing higher education provides you with knowledge, connections, and opportunities you would never have had without proper schooling. This is well worth any exams you might have to take.

8. LOOK FOR NEW EXPERIENCES

While a formal education is a great place to start, there is no better way to learn than by doing. Do not allow fear to hinder you from trying something new. Branch out and seek to learn skills outside of your desired field. These skill sets can prove to be extremely beneficial in the long run in unexpected ways. As you engage in new experiences, you will broaden your skillset and learn so much more. For example, you can travel to a new country to look for work opportunities, further your education, or engage in new leisure activities. If you haven't visited the rural parts of your country, do so. Or even vice versa! Try a cuisine outside of your tradition. Pursue something you've always had an interest in doing but never had the guts to do. New experiences will definitely help you to expand your horizons and live a more gratifying life. To experience a bit more enthusiasm, acquire new viewpoints, and keep life fascinating, you ought to look for and engage in new experiences.

"A mind that is stretched by a new experience can never go back to its old dimensions."

— *OLIVER WENDELL HOLMES, JR.*

---

9. GET ORGANIZED

Disorganization can drastically slow down your working speed. If you have to spend the first ten minutes of every study or work session trying to find where you left a particular folder, you're wasting time. Create and stick to an organizational system. You can purchase a journal, or just an ordinary notebook, to keep a log of things you need to remember. It is wise to assign every material thing you own a place of its own; this lets you know where items might be located. You need to ensure that your space remains organized, so including some time to re-organize when things get cluttered, or just out of order, will be a plus for you. This will save you far more time in the long run than you spend in the initial organizing process.

10. RESPECT YOUR ELDERS

Having respect for my elders is one regulation my granny ensured I obeyed. Your elders can teach you so much about the world. They can provide guidance when you are unsure of what to do next. You can learn things the easy way that they had to learn the hard way. Heed their advice, even if your gut reaction is to disagree. Trust that their experiences are worth listening to, and you will acquire an abundance of knowledge you weren't aware of.

11. CULTIVATE GOOD HABITS

Bad habits are hard to stop, but that's precisely why you need to put an end to them. Rid your life of anything that wastes your time or harms your physical or mental health. This includes, but is not limited to, excessive drinking, smoking, drugs, partying, and staying up all night on the weekends. Instead, drink plenty of water, eat healthily, and rest. Be open to nurturing a mindset that welcomes other good habits that will improve the quality of your life. To do this, you need to learn to resist the temptation to revert back to bad habits and outline the good practices you want to cultivate. These are two of several ways in which to accomplish this mission. Not only will your body feel better, but your mind will too. You will feel refreshed instead of groggy in the morning, and you will be more productive throughout the day.

12. MASTER THE ART OF LISTENING

Pay attention! We spend a lot of time talking, but we don't always spend much time listening. We might get so wrapped up in our own excitement that we forget we don't have all the answers. If we spend more time listening, we'll hear valuable advice that we might have missed out on. We'll also become better at considering others' ideas rather than stubbornly insisting on our own, which can save us from making some less-than-stellar decisions.

13. ADDRESS YOUR WEAK SPOTS

Everyone has weak points and areas where they struggle. These areas require a bit more attention than the ones we excel in. Allowing a particular skill to fall by the wayside only makes the weak spot worsen over time. If you are not good at Math and choose to focus on all the other subjects, refusing to practice on your own or get help, you're setting yourself up to fail! Addressing your weak spots early and improving your skills in those areas will help you avoid future fallout.

14. BECOME MORE CONFIDENT

Like a lack of self-esteem and self-efficacy, a lack of confidence can hold us back. It can prevent us from trying new things and encourage us to stick to what we know. This limits the amount that we can learn and makes it harder to take advantage of good opportunities when they appear. Visualizing yourself as what you want to be and deliberately affirming that you will achieve what you set out to accomplish are two powerful actions to becoming a more confident person. The best suggestion of all is to not let negative, insensitive comments hit you hard. You do know what's true about you, so let who you are shine through your confidence. As your confidence grows, you will find it easier to do things that would have made you freeze up before. Besides, this confidence boost will open many new pathways for you, enable you to take charge of your emotions, and help you overcome obstacles.

15. LEARN HOW TO BE A PUBLIC SPEAKER

Developing your public speaking skills is an extension of becoming more confident. Being an effective speaker requires confidence to face the crowd, but it also requires excellent communication skills. Take a public speaking class or seminar, or practice speaking skills in front of small audiences, slowly working your way up to larger ones. You will become an efficient communicator in no time.

16. CHOOSE HAPPINESS

Frankly speaking, if your current life is making you miserable, something needs to change. If you're not enjoying your life, you're going to have trouble remaining motivated. All of your self-investment efforts will annoy and frustrate you rather than elevate you. Decide to pursue your happiness, even when it means leaving a comfortable lifestyle for a more uncertain one. The change will be worth it when you can genuinely say you are happy.

17. DEVELOP EMOTIONAL INTELLIGENCE

Emotional intelligence is just as relevant as other forms of education. If you are emotionally intelligent, you have an easier time understanding what others are feeling and your own feelings. This makes you better at resolving conflicts. It can make you a better salesperson too, as you can read people and understand how they feel about the idea you're pitching them. Emotional intelligence will also help you maintain personal relationships with fewer arguments as you start to see things from someone else's point of view.

18. EMBRACE GROWTH

You always have the chance to grow. You can always learn new skills and improve your character, no matter your age or what you've been through in life. The ideology that you're too old to change something about your life, or that you're too young to worry about your future is a failure's creed. You are not a failure! Embrace growth in all its forms and keep striving to be the best version of yourself.

19. INVEST IN HIGHLY MARKETABLE SKILLS

There are several valuable skills in a variety of industries. For example, excellent communication skills will help you just about anywhere. It can also make you a better salesperson. When you can market your ideas, or even yourself, you get a huge leg up over the competition. Other highly marketable skills include knowledge of analytics, problem-solving skills, and proficiency with technology. These kinds of skills will come up in the vast majority of jobs, and being able to put them on your resume makes you a better candidate.

20. INVEST IN YOUR HEALTH AND ENERGY

Your energy is your greatest asset, so you should be sure to maintain it. This means looking out for your physical and mental health. Go to bed on time, eat a balanced diet, get some exercise, and take time off when you need it. All of these things ensure you will have enough energy to work on any task.

21. EXPAND YOUR NETWORK

Networking isn't just about meeting as many people as possible. It's about building a community full of like-minded people who want to help each other succeed. It would help if you had a network with a few people pursuing similar goals. It should be a positive and encouraging group. Huge networks where it is impossible to know people personally or those that breed negativity can quickly get out of hand without actually providing any benefits to you. Know your limits.

22. FIND A MENTOR

If you want to learn how to do something, ask someone who has done it before. Mentors are a fantastic resource. Look for someone who is living the kind of life you want for yourself. They are best equipped to advise you on where to focus your efforts to achieve that life. The advice and assistance that mentors provide are invaluable.

At age nineteen, on my quest to find guidance and constructive feedback on my personal and professional development journeys, I discovered my mentor—Sir Laing. His training in theater arts, public relations, and community development certainly helped to facilitate a more fulfilling and beneficial network between us. This tango-type relationship shaped my life for the better. He ensured I understood that as a mentee, I needed to model positive attitudes and behaviors, without which my success under his tutelage would be defeated. Sir Laing was the one who recommended that I reduce my resume from an accomplishment-packed five pages. On May 16, 2014, he said in an email:

"This needs to be reviewed; five pages is way too much, Michael. Even professionals are not encouraged to go beyond two pages. Please make the effort to review with a view to [condense] what you have..."

— *EJ*

Another noteworthy moment in our mentor-mentee relationship was when Mr. Laing encouraged me to autograph all my work with excellence. He was proud of the accomplishments I'd already made, but he was even more thrilled to guide, advise, and support me toward achieving much more. He taught me how to leverage my morals, talents, and strengths. In some ways, and now several years later, I still find myself trying to measure up to what my mentor, Sir Laing, expected of me.

"Mentoring is a brain to pick, an ear to listen, and a push in the right direction."

— JOHN C. CROSBY

---

23. CREATE A VISION BOARD

Finally, make a vision board. This involves creating a collage highlighting several things you want to achieve in the future. Your vision board helps you identify your goals, and it puts them front and center in your mind every time you see it. When you visualize your goals and always think about them, following through on them and eventually achieving them becomes much more manageable.

I created my first vision board on a large sheet of black cartridge paper in January of 2012, a few days shy of my eighteenth birthday. The inspiration to do so stemmed from a 4-H Club seminar I attended. On that board, which was completely abstract, several newspaper cutouts overlapped. I remember ripping the Head Boy badge from a young man's chest in the Gleaner—a Jamaican morning daily broadsheet—and pasting it onto my vision board, alongside pictures of the Edna Manley College of the Visual and Performing Arts, The University of the West Indies, Mona, and Willard Carroll Smith Jr., popularly known as Will Smith—my all-time favorite actor and comedian. That vision board helped me actualize and achieve my goals of obtaining leadership positions in secondary school and pursuing higher education thereafter. It has also propelled me to make significant progress toward my aim to become a professional actor. Though this board has been destroyed, its contents are still etched in my mind. Besides, I've created a much more advanced vision board, reflecting adulthood milestones.

"Your brain will work tirelessly to achieve the statements you give your subconscious mind. And when those statements are the affirmations and images of your goals, you are destined to achieve them!"

— JACK CANFIELD

12

SELF-MADE

DRAFTING YOUR "SELF-INVESTMENT STATEMENT"

When you write a self-investment statement, you give yourself greater clarity on the things you want to accomplish, and you hold yourself accountable for achieving them.

As we draw close to the end of the book, this chapter will challenge you to a self-investment activity. In earlier chapters, we spoke about the importance of setting goals and making a plan for yourself. A clear and coherent plan will take you from point A to point B. It will outline all the steps you need to complete in order to achieve success. Now, you're going to make a personal self-investment statement so you can proceed with a revitalized self-investment quest. If you effectively complete this chapter's activity, it is only fitting that self-made success stories will attract to your life.

Self-made is a term used to describe when a person acquires success through their own efforts. Often you hear of the term self-made millionaires. You can achieve this kind of success in your self-investment pursuits if you digest and actualize all you've learned from this book. The way you process the information will help you create and outline your overarching mission statement. This statement will be a concrete plan for your life. It should be written to enact who you become, what you become, and your reason for wanting to be this person. Though the plan is described as concrete, you should be able to revise it as time and your desires change. This is how you implement and maintain the self-made practice.

The outline you make for yourself should be similar to an investment policy statement: "A document drafted between a portfolio manager and a client" that "provides the general investment goals and objectives of a client and describes the strategies that the manager should employ to meet these objectives" (Kagan, 2020c, para. 1). Essentially, the investment policy statement is a contract that lays out what goals need to be achieved and how the portfolio manager plans to achieve them. It prevents people from making snap decisions that are not aligned with their intended interests, and it gives everyone involved with the investment a clear strategy to follow.

With that in mind, you are now going to write down and vocalize your personal self-investment statement in the form of a mission statement, one that follows the same goals as the investment policy statement. You've probably heard of mission statements in the context of multimillion-dollar companies, but they're not the only ones who can use mission statements to their advantage. You can also use a mission statement to guide the decisions you make later on in life. Once you have a mission statement in place, you can break goals into smaller milestones and tackle each of them, knowing you're contributing to your overall intents. When you write a self-investment statement, you give yourself greater clarity on the things you want to accomplish, and you hold yourself accountable for achieving them.

"Goals in writing are dreams with deadlines."

— BRIAN TRACY

Another great reason to get your mission statement written out right away is that it's a good way to measure your progress and how invested you are in making that progress. Ideally, you would know precisely what you want to accomplish in life from day one, so you could spend your whole existence working toward it. However, that's just not how things work. The job I wanted when I was five years old isn't the job I want now, and the future life I envisioned for myself a decade ago is definitely not in line with what I currently value. My interests grew and changed over time. My goals inevitably changed too.

If, later on, you find that your mission statement has things you are not actually interested in anymore, simply adjust your trajectory until you're aiming for goals that align with your interests and values. Sometimes, you get to keep and repurpose the progress you've made so far. Sometimes, you don't get so lucky. If you end up needing to scrap everything and start from scratch, moving in an entirely different direction, be thankful that you're still alive because you have more than enough time to be indecisive. Move to follow your heart's desire, wherever it ends up taking you.

HOW TO IDENTIFY YOUR MISSION STATEMENT

You know why a mission statement matters; now, you need to know how to make one. Luckily, the process is not nearly as complicated as it sounds. You simply need to identify your most important belief and the outcome you most want to see from your self-investment efforts. Think about the long-term goals you want to achieve, not just the short-term ones. Your mission statement should also be inspiring enough to remind you what you're fighting for when you face obstacles and hardships. You want to have a clear reason for refusing to give up, and your mission statement should provide you with precisely that.

When crafting your mission statement, you want to avoid any overly generic goals. It's best to set specific goals that are as personal as possible. We discussed this in an earlier chapter, but just to review, the goals you set for yourself should be relevant and measurable. They should appeal to you, or they won't be very useful motivators. If your mission statement is too generic, it doesn't help you create a self-investment statement at all because it doesn't represent you.

> *"Without goals, and plans to reach them, you are like a ship that has set sail with no destination."*
>
> — FITZHUGH DODSON

Now let's take a look at the two strategies I focused on mastering on my self-investment journey. These approaches can assist you in drafting an effective mission statement that outlines your moral self, goals, and purpose in life.

SELF-REFLECTION AND VISUALIZATION

We've touched briefly on the benefits of self-reflection and visualization before. Now we'll examine specific forward-thinking exercises you can use to visualize what success entails for you.

You can understand a lot about yourself and what matters to you if you take a moment to reflect on your perfect life. When you think about your future, what do you see? What kind of lifestyle would you live if you had no restrictions? Can you see yourself in any particular career? The life you visualize as your perfect future is exactly what your goals should help you achieve.

Once you've let yourself daydream for a bit, think about the things that helped make your dream future perfect. You can write these down if you like. Then, write down the smaller goals that will help you manifest these things from your dreams into reality. If you have a specific job in mind, research and write down the steps you'd need to take and the skills you'd need to learn for that job. Do the same for other aspects of your dream lifestyle until you have a complete plan for achieving everything you desire. From here, you can identify smaller goals to work toward that will help you reach your larger goals later.

CONSIDERING CORE VALUES

The life you lead should be in tune with the values that matter most to you. What kind of values do you admire in others? Which values do you most want to see in yourself? Building the perfect future isn't just about making sure you achieve material wealth; it also means making sure you live a life you can feel good about.

You can develop these values in yourself just the same as you would develop any skill. Write down ways you could get more practice expressing positive values. You can also write down how practicing these values improves your life and the lives of those around you. This way, you have a clear idea of the values you want to adapt and why they matter. This provides you with the motivation you need to stick to your values, even when it might be easier to achieve material success less morally.

At this point, you probably have a pretty good idea of what your mission statement should be. You also know everything you need to do to achieve it. Let's take a moment to examine an extract from my mission statement.

A SNIPPET OF MY CURRENT MISSION STATEMENT

My mission is to be guided in life by
honesty, integrity, and mutual respect for all.
To never lose sight of the bigger picture.
To constantly aim toward
consciously actualizing the best version of me—
academically, professionally, and spiritually.
And to capitalize on the power
of my voice and experiences
to inspire others alike.
My dream is to be known
as an accomplished
lecturer, actor, author, and entrepreneur
by the age of thirty-five.
I can do this!
I will find impetus in me.
I will believe in me.
I will support me.
I will have discipline.
I will seek help when I need it most.
For me, I will conquer all odds
to accomplish what I envision to be
my victory.

I deliberately extracted this portion of text from my mission statement to solidify the importance of ethics, long-term goals, and a desire to succeed. The core ethical values that I selected to be guided by as I continue to learn, grow, and glow are honesty, integrity, and mutual respect for all. I decided to be guided by *honesty* because to create a clear roadmap to actualize my best self, I need to be brutally honest with myself and the people with whom I interact. *Integrity* is a trait I deem beneficial because it has constantly navigated my thoughts around negative energies and has enabled me to do the right thing in several instances. I've heard my grandmother reiterate the famous saying, *"respect is a two-way street,"* too many times. Hence my acknowledgment and quest to continuously *respect* everyone no matter what differentiates me from them.

I am motivated never to lose sight of the bigger picture. This statement guides me to envision my future life whenever I need to make critical choices. It stops me from making a serious error in judgment about my life's most major decisions. Essentially, it reminds me to connect the dots as I make decisions in my ever-evolving life. *To never lose sight of the bigger picture* illustrates an account of every aspect in my life that my decisions will affect—the current me and my future self.

To constantly aim toward consciously actualizing the best version of me... articulates my yearn to undergo constant transformation deliberately. The truth is, we only can get better and better each day. The 4-H motto specifically inspires me to make my best better, endlessly. I aim to improve and offer my best self in academic, professional, and spiritual realms. As I grow and glow up, I plan to share my experiences as much as possible, hoping that they may inspire others to be better versions of themselves.

The professions I listed in my mission statement are four of my long-term goals. I've already started to earn developmental dividends that will spur me toward accomplishing each of them by my self-imposed deadline—age thirty-five. This deadline, and others, help to create a sense of urgency which propels me to work toward my goals more efficiently.

In my mission statement, I chose to include six affirmative statements, five of which are: *I can do this! I will find impetus in me. I will believe in me. I will support me. I will have discipline.* I specifically selected these statements because they have been the words of encouragement I periodically use when I decide to tackle difficult tasks. I repeat them with intentions to reprogram my unconscious mind for success. They are powerful words. They overshadow my fears and doubts by infiltrating drive, confidence, certainty, and self-control in me.

The final reaffirming statement is at the end of my mission statement. It serves as a reminder to fight to overcome all obstacles and hardships for my sake. I will choose not to walk away from difficulties; I will lean into them to reap the benefit of actualizing a stronger and more rigid self. *For me, I will conquer all odds to accomplish what I envision to be my victory.*

Asking for help is not a bad thing. Often, we pride ourselves on accomplishing things on our own without help. Thus, we fail to recognize that we have clear-thinking friends we can confide in—

friends who will drive a tractor through our wide-eyed presumptions. In the past, I would try to do everything by myself. Over time, I've learned there is no shame in asking for help. So, I've decided that *I will seek help when I need it most.* If I am stuck in the problem-solving phase or unable to execute a task because I lack a certain skill, I will seek help. I will forever ask for help when it is undoubtedly necessary.

My statement is not too overly generic. It identifies three core values I want to radiate in all my interactions. It highlights the three realms in my life I want to excel in. And it has four specific goals I plan to accomplish and a deadline for which I hold myself accountable. My mission statement also has humble affirmative statements.

When you write your self-investment mission statement, focus on the things that matter most to you. There is no need for intricate language. It needs to be simple and to the point. Make it super, super specific! I challenge you to take a few minutes, hours, or even days, to envisage and pen your mission statement.

Feel free to share them with me via email or social media.

#missionstatementwritten

All that's left is for you to take the plunge, follow the path laid out for you by your mission statement, and start to bank on self-investment.

13

SELF-UPGRADE

"WITHDRAWING" FROM RECURRING ACCOUNTS OF SUCCESS

To withdraw from your self-investment accounts is to collect on and enjoy all the benefits your hard work has gotten you.

Banking on self-investment is the best thing you can do for yourself to ensure long-term success. You invest very early on, but you don't get to see the rewards right away. It takes effort, time, and continual reinvesting. Eventually, all of this hard work will pay off. Your commitment to your goals and your belief in your capabilities will lead you to the future you want for yourself. When you finally get there, it will be all the sweeter for the amount of work you put in.

Regular bank accounts and investment accounts often undergo an upgrade based on customer preference. Like those accounts, you, too, need an upgrade at certain points in time. At this step in your self-investment journey, you need to rely heavily on your drive to continue to aim for bigger and better milestones—this is what it means to self-upgrade. Ensure that you are upgrading your motivation, enthusiasm, creativity, and overall personal prospectus. Your self-upgrade should be cyclic. It is up to you to be more self-confident, self-assured, well-informed, and well-mannered to be able to achieve your greatest goals.

Everything we have reviewed up to this point involves making deposits into yourself—which was theorized as an investment account. Now, at last, you get to enjoy the results of all of your deposits. When you look at the account—that is yourself—you will find that you are overflowing with the fruits of your labor, which you now get to reap. You can cash out on all the success you've accomplished—this is your triumph withdrawn. To withdraw from your self-investment accounts is to collect on and enjoy all the benefits from your hard work. When you deposit belief in yourself to contest fear and to persevere amidst challenges, the end result will inevitably be triumph withdrawn.

WHAT IT MEANS TO WITHDRAW TRIUMPH

The withdrawing triumph stage of self-investment is the culmination of all of your efforts. At this point, you get to cash in on all of the investments you've made. This might mean different things, depending on the goals you set for yourself. Maybe you're doing well academically, and you're well on your way to furthering your education. You might have a new job you enjoy. Perhaps you've expanded your social circle. You have probably developed many new skills, and you've given yourself a great mindset that will help you deal with obstacles in all their forms. Withdrawn triumph could look like any or all of these goals and improvements. The most important thing is that you are cashing in on promises you've made to yourself.

When you started investing in yourself, you created a pact. You said you would put in the effort and energy, and in exchange, you would see results. You now get to see that the pact you made paid off, and you are getting the results you always hoped for. You might have even surpassed your initial goals, which is an amazing feat. When you withdraw triumph, you get to enjoy your success and take pride in everything you did to get to this point.

WHAT'S NEXT?

What's left to do once you find success and achieve your goals? If you're used to working toward the same goal for a long time, you might be a little uncertain about what you should do after you finally achieve it.

First off, take a moment to celebrate.

"Allow yourself to be proud of yourself and all the progress you've made. Especially the progress that no one else has seen."

— *ANONYMOUS ON INSTAGRAM*

When you win at first, celebrate. Yes. You've more than earned it! But, do not allow your celebration to power your ego too much. Make time to spend a few hours, days, or a week relaxing and not thinking about future projects. This keeps you from getting burned out. It also allows some of the initial rush of excitement to die down so you can make decisions for the future with a clear head.

Once you're calmer and clearheaded, you can decide what your next goal should be. Achieving your initial goals is excellent, but don't stop there. Appreciate your successes and allow them to form part of your motivation to achieve even larger goals. As you reach greater success, more opportunities will open up to you. Make the most of these opportunities just like you did for the previous ones and reinvest in yourself.

CONCLUSION

You get out of your life an amount proportional to what you put into it. This is why it is so important to invest in yourself. If you back away from countless opportunities, you never give yourself a chance to grow. You don't get to test your skills, nor do you get enough practice and experience to expand these skills. If you are too worried about the possibility of failure to ever try something out of your comfort zone, you limit your ability to succeed.

Investing can be scary because there's no guarantee you will achieve the kind of success you're dreaming of. But if you never make an attempt in the first place, you will never give yourself the chance to succeed. When investors purchase stocks, there's no guarantee they'll make their money back. If the stock abruptly tanks in value, they might lose everything they spent. Yet, they invest anyway. When you invest in yourself, you make a much safer bet. Your efforts cannot go to waste, because no matter how much success you achieve, you have still put in the work to become a better version of yourself. You always improve when you self-invest, which makes it always worth doing. If people can knowingly enter into the high-risk world of the stock market, then there's no reason why you can't choose to invest in yourself.

In order to succeed, the most important value to cultivate is self-discipline. Discipline is the prerequisite of all forms of success. It represents the bridge between the goals in your mind and actually achieving them in the real world. You could read every productivity and self-help book in the world, but if you never follow the steps they've outlined for you, then you might as well have not read them at all. Nothing will change in your life if you don't take action, and that requires discipline.

"We don't have to be smarter than the rest, we have to be more disciplined than the rest."

— WARREN BUFFETT

This is the place where most people fail. They shut the book, place it on their bookshelf, or just toss it wherever really, and never act on anything inside. Break that cycle! Master self-discipline so you can get down to work right away and execute everything you've learned so far. When you're disciplined, you won't hesitate to invest because you know that a little discomfort and uncertainty can lead to amazing things.

> *"You have to start taking action, learning from those actions —whether you succeed or fail—and improving until you get it right"* (Graziosi, 2019, p. 89).

Remember that investments need time to increase in value, so don't delay any longer. Start drafting your self-investment statement today so you can experience all the long-term benefits sooner rather than later. The earlier you start, the faster you will see results, and the more time you will give your self-investment to really pay off.

As humans, we are exceptional storytellers. We make sense of and add meaning to our past experiences using very descriptive narratives. These narratives become the actual structure of the stories we tell ourselves and the lived realities we create, often involuntarily. Discovering the power of your own experiences and sifting through how they've impacted who you are today will motivate you to craft more empowering stories that charter progression toward a better future. At this moment, your full self will flourish, even as you continue on your self-investment journey.

Have faith in you! You can lead the life you want for yourself and achieve the success you've been searching for. When you bank on self-investment, you can withdraw triumph—just work, work, work on you, and believe.

If you found this book to be incredibly useful, consider giving it a review online. This helps others to learn about the amazing power of self-investment and how they can use it to become the best version of themselves, just as you have.

You can also spread the message using
#stimuluscheckcompleted
on social media.

REFERENCES

Aronson, B. (n.d.). *Famous failures: 23 stories to inspire you to succeed.* https://www.bradaronson.com/famous-failures/

Bandura, A. (1994). Self-efficacy. *Encyclopedia of Human Behavior,* 4, 71-81. https://www.uky.edu/~eushe2/Bandura/Bandura1994EHB.pdf

Chen, J. (2020, July 18). *Guide to dividend investing.* Investopedia. https://www.investopedia.com/terms/d/dividend.asp

Graziosi, D. (2019). The underdog advantage. Rewrite your future by turning your disadvantages into your superpowers. BBG Publishing.

Kagan, J. (2020a, Mar. 9). *Collateral.* Investopedia. https://www.investopedia.com/terms/c/collateral.asp

Kagan, J. (2020b, Mar. 18). *Financial plan.* Investopedia. https://www.investopedia.com/terms/f/financial_plan.asp

Kagan, J. (2020c, May 25). *Investment policy statement (IPS).* Investopedia. https://www.investopedia.com/terms/i/ips.asp

Kagan, J. (2020d, Apr. 20). *Overdraft.* Investopedia. https://www.investopedia.com/terms/o/overdraft.asp

Kuffel, H. (2019, Oct. 2). *What is a prospectus and how do you read one?* SmartAsset. https://smartasset.com/investing/prospectus

Porter, J. (2017, Mar. 21). *Why you should make time for self-reflection (Even if you hate it).* Harvard Business Review. https://hbr.org/2017/03/why-you-should-make-time-for-self-reflection-even-if-you-hate-doing-it

Sáez, F. (n.d.). *Micro-tasks: The pleasure of checking off.* FacileThings. https://facilethings.com/blog/en/micro-tasks

Tomlinson, K. (2018). Kill fear. The art of courageous living. Self-Pub., Kingston, Jamaica.

www.ingramcontent.com/pod-product-compliance
Lightning Source LLC
Chambersburg PA
CBHW030344190426
43201CB00042B/407